4/2/01 Baker + Saylor 22.96.

READINGS ON

FAHRENHEIT 451

THE GREENHAVEN PRESS
Literary Companion
TO AMERICAN LITERATURE

FAHRENHEIT 451

Katie de Koster, *Book Editor*

David L. Bender, *Publisher*
Bruno Leone, *Executive Editor*
Bonnie Szumski, *Series Editor*

Greenhaven Press, Inc., San Diego, CA

813
ReA

Every effort has been made to trace the owners of copy-righted material. The articles in this volume may have been edited for content, length, and/or reading level. The titles have been changed to enhance the editorial purpose. Those interested in locating the original source will find the complete citation on the first page of each article.

12439

Library of Congress Cataloging-in-Publication Data

Readings on Fahrenheit 451 /Katie de Koster, book editor.
        p.   cm. — (The Greenhaven Press literary
    companion to American literature)
        Includes bibliographical references (p.   ) and index.
        ISBN 1-56510-856-6 (pbk. : alk. paper). —
    ISBN 1-56510-857-4 (lib. : alk. paper)
        1. Bradbury, Ray, 1920–   Fahrenheit 451.
    2. Book burning in literature. I. de Koster, Katie, 1948–   .
    II. Series.
    PS3503.R167F337   2000
    813'.54—dc21   99-38379
                                                            CIP

Cover photo: Photofest

> *Go to the edge of the cliff and jump off. Build your wings on the way down.*

—*Ray Bradbury*

CONTENTS

Chapter 1: Symbol and Metaphor in *Fahrenheit 451*

Chapter 2: Dystopia and Utopia

vides a stark contrast to the deeper values Montag develops
over the course of the novel.

Chapter 3: A Reflection of the Real World

FOREWORD

*"'Tis the good reader that
makes the good book."*

Ralph Waldo Emerson

The story's bare facts are simple: The captain, an old and scarred seafarer, walks with a peg leg made of whale ivory. He relentlessly drives his crew to hunt the world's oceans for the great white whale that crippled him. After a long search, the ship encounters the whale and a fierce battle ensues. Finally the captain drives his harpoon into the whale, but the harpoon line catches the captain about the neck and drags him to his death.

A simple story, a straightforward plot—yet, since the 1851 publication of Herman Melville's *Moby-Dick*, readers and critics have found many meanings in the struggle between Captain Ahab and the whale. To some, the novel is a cautionary tale that depicts how Ahab's obsession with revenge leads to his insanity and death. Others believe that the whale represents the unknowable secrets of the universe and that Ahab is a tragic hero who dares to challenge fate by attempting to discover this knowledge. Perhaps Melville intended Ahab as a criticism of Americans' tendency to become involved in well-intentioned but irrational causes. Or did Melville model Ahab after himself, letting his fictional character express his anger at what he perceived as a cruel and distant god?

Although literary critics disagree over the meaning of *Moby-Dick*, readers do not need to choose one particular interpretation in order to gain an understanding of Melville's

8

novel. Instead, by examining various analyses, they can gain numerous insights into the issues that lie under the surface of the basic plot. Studying the writings of literary critics can also aid readers in making their own assessments of *Moby-Dick* and other literary works and in developing analytical thinking skills.

The Greenhaven Literary Companion Series was created with these goals in mind. Designed for young adults, this unique anthology series provides an engaging and comprehensive introduction to literary analysis and criticism. The essays included in the Literary Companion Series are chosen for their accessibility to a young adult audience and are expertly edited in consideration of both the reading and comprehension levels of this audience. In addition, each essay is introduced by a concise summation that presents the contributing writer's main themes and insights. Every anthology in the Literary Companion Series contains a varied selection of critical essays that cover a wide time span and express diverse views. Wherever possible, primary sources are represented through excerpts from authors' notebooks, letters, and journals and through contemporary criticism.

Each title in the Literary Companion Series pays careful consideration to the historical context of the particular author or literary work. In-depth biographies and detailed chronologies reveal important aspects of authors' lives and emphasize the historical events and social milieu that influenced their writings. To facilitate further research, every anthology includes primary and secondary source bibliographies of articles and/or books selected for their suitability for young adults. These engaging features make the Greenhaven Literary Companion series ideal for introducing students to literary analysis in the classroom or as a library resource for young adults researching the world's great authors and literature.

Exceptional in its focus on young adults, the Greenhaven Literary Companion Series strives to present literary criticism in a compelling and accessible format. Every title in the series is intended to spark readers' interest in leading American and world authors, to help them broaden their understanding of literature, and to encourage them to formulate their own analyses of the literary works that they read. It is the editors' hope that young adult readers will find these anthologies to be true companions in their study of literature.

INTRODUCTION

In his book *Seekers of Tomorrow*, Sam Moskowitz writes that when Ray Bradbury was young, he advocated a political philosophy called technocracy, which predicted that the national economy was going to collapse in 1945. At that point a group of technocrats calling themselves Technocracy, Inc. (TI), would step forward and a series of appointed scientists would run the country according to scientific principles. Bradbury was later horrified to discover that TI was involved in Nazi book burning in Europe (a zealous attempt to enforce Nazi "scientific" principles). As an author, he took book burning personally, as he suggests in these lines from *Fahrenheit 451:*

> "It's not just the woman that died," said Montag. "Last night I thought about all the kerosene that I've used in the past ten years. And I thought about books. And for the first time I realized that a man was behind each one of the books. A man had to think them up. A man had to take a long time to put them down on paper."

Thus Bradbury used what was, to him, the horrific idea of book burning in his novel *Fahrenheit 451* in response to another horrific situation: the persecutions resulting from a fear of communism (the Red scare) that gripped the nation at midcentury.

THE RED SCARE

Although the USSR had been an ally during World War II, relations between that country and the West had been tense since the Bolshevik Revolution (1918–1921) that followed World War I. As first the USSR and then China adopted the relatively new political philosophy of communism, it seemed the world would eventually devolve into two massive armed camps: the communists and the anticommunists. The communists, however, were not all overseas. The American Communist Party hoped to replace democracy and capitalism with communism within the United States. Today, with the benefit of hindsight, this political ideology may seem sinister, but the stated goals of communism appealed to many idealistic people. Communists advocated an equitable sharing of wealth; the idea that those who did the work, rather than those who only supplied the money, should control the tools of production and profits; and a philosophy of protecting the weak. Early supporters were joined by others who deplored what they saw as American imperialism, attempts to become involved in or control the affairs of foreign countries and to annex territory outside the geographical boundaries of the United States, a widespread policy among industrialized countries since the turn of the century.

Meanwhile, the political situation in Europe in the late 1930s became increasingly volatile. In 1938, shortly before World War II began, the U.S. House of Representatives established a committee to investigate "un-American" activities among the country's citizens. Originally it investigated what it considered suspicious activities of those from both the political left and the political right. By 1947, however, when the House Un-American Activities Committee (HUAC) opened hearings on suspected communist infiltration of Hollywood, only those on the political left had anything to fear from the committee.

And "fear" is the appropriate word. The committee was determined to expose and discredit anyone in a position to advance the communist cause in the powerful entertainment industry, and accusations were abundant, often with little or no evidence. A series of "unfriendly witnesses" were called before the committee and asked to acknowledge that they were communists and to name fellow communists. When they refused to name "fellow travelers," several were jailed, and many were blackballed by the major Hollywood studios. This year, 1947, is when Bradbury—who lived in Los Angeles and had many friends in Hollywood—wrote "The Phoenix," the seed story that would become *Fahrenheit 451*.

In 1950, Senator Joseph McCarthy—taking advantage of the growing animosity between East and West—proclaimed, "Today we are engaged in a final, all-out battle between communistic atheism and Christianity." McCarthy sponsored hearings in the Senate similar to those conducted by HUAC, but they were aimed at more diverse targets, from congressmen to high-ranking military officers. These hearings were prosecuted with such vigor and acrimony that the Wisconsin senator gave his name to the modern witch hunt: "Mc-

Carthyism," personal attacks on individuals by means of widely publicized indiscriminate allegations, especially on the basis of unsubstantiated charges. In February 1951, Bradbury's story "The Fireman" (a sort of middle stage between "The Phoenix" and *Fahrenheit 451*) was published.

CRITICIZING THE HYSTERIA

The charged atmosphere created by powerful figures such as McCarthy made it dangerous to speak out directly against the persecution, but many artists found ways to condemn the fears and injustice. Arthur Miller's play *The Crucible*, for example, debuted on Broadway in 1953, the same year *Fahrenheit 451* was published. This powerful drama takes as its overt subject the Salem witch trials of 1692, but the underlying message is about the destruction of innocent people when fear, hysteria, and indiscriminate accusations rule–a not-too-subtle attack on McCarthyism.

Bradbury's book is a slightly more oblique attack, although he has stated that he did intend it as a criticism of McCarthyism. In *Fahrenheit 451* he mourns not only the government's determination to tell people what to think and to destroy those who show any signs of independent thought, but the people's willingness to stop thinking—and reading—for themselves.

Book burning and repression of thought and ideas are far from the only themes in *Fahrenheit 451*. The novel comments on many other aspects of modern life that Bradbury deplores, and it is a striking vindication of his vision that many of the aspects of modern life he deplored a half-century ago are even more pronounced today.

Ray Bradbury: A Biography

Ray Bradbury will tell you that he remembers being born, and he remembers having nightmares about the trauma of birth for several weeks afterward. He writes, in the introduction to *The Ray Bradbury Companion:*

> I have what might be called almost total recall back to the hour of my birth. I remember suckling, circumcision, and nightmares-about-being-born experienced in my crib in the first weeks of my life. Most people don't remember. Psychologists say that babies are born undeveloped, and that only after some few days and weeks are they capable of seeing, hearing, knowing. But, I saw, I heard, I knew. And, later in my life, wrote a story about myself called "The Small Assassin," in which a child is born fully aware and sets out to revenge itself on its parents for having thrust it into the world.

Memories, dreams, and the ability to transform personal experience into tales of universal relevance are critical elements in Bradbury's art, an alchemy he practices daily in his chosen profession of mythmaker.

A Midwestern Childhood

Bradbury's first traumatic experience, being born, took place August 22, 1920, in Waukegan, Illinois. Raymond Douglas Bradbury (the middle name was his parents' salute to actor Douglas Fairbanks) was the third son of Leonard Spaulding Bradbury and Esther Marie Moberg Bradbury.

Ray's father was descended from an English family that immigrated to America in 1630. As his son Ray would be, Leonard's father and grandfather had been in the word business: as Bradbury and Son, they had published two Illinois newspapers. Leonard, however, ran away from home to live in Tucson, Arizona, when he was sixteen. When he returned to Waukegan, he did not join the family enterprise, opting instead to work as a telephone lineman for the Waukegan Bureau of Power and Light.

Bradbury does not mention his father often. In his introduction to the 1975 edition of *Dandelion Wine*, he wrote, "I
was a boy who did indeed love his parents and grandparents
and brother," but the dedication to his short-story collection
A Medicine for Melancholy reads, "For Dad, whose love, very
late in life, surprised his son."

Bradbury's mother, Esther Marie Moberg, was born in
Stockholm, Sweden, and immigrated with her family to
Massachusetts at the age of two. When she was eight, her
family moved to Waukegan, where she met and married
Leonard after his return from his youthful foray in Arizona.
In his introduction to *They Came from Outer Space*, Bradbury
has lovingly described her as "a maniac mother who had to
be dragged from silent movie theaters, after late matinees, by
a hungry husband or a son sent to fetch mama home. More
often than not the son forgot when he had come and stayed
with mom for one more rerun." He loved the "delicious
fright" movies gave him, but wrote in *Weird Tales* in November 1943,

> Some of my first memories concern going upstairs at night
> and finding an unpleasant beast waiting at the next to the last
> step. Screaming, I'd run back down to mother. Then, together,
> we'd climb the stairs. Invariably, the monster would be gone.
> Mother never saw it. Sometimes I was irritated at her lack of
> imagination.

Esther and Leonard's first children were twin sons,
Leonard and Samuel, born in 1916. Samuel died at age two,
so when Ray was born two years later, he had one older
brother, an athletic lad who would later be nicknamed Skip.
Unlike his brother, Ray (nicknamed Shorty) did not become
one of the "muscle people," as he called them, but instead developed into a dreamer with a pocketful of passions for Buck
Rogers, Tarzan, scary movies, traveling carnivals, and magi-
cians.

Waukegan, in Bradbury's memory, was the perfect place
to grow up, an old-fashioned place that he calls Green Town
in his "autobiographical fantasy" books, *Dandelion Wine* and
Something Wicked This Way Comes. It was a place of friends
and extended family, front porches and traveling carnivals,
barefoot summers and swimming in the lake. Ray would
dress up as a vampire bat, hang upside down from trees, and
drop onto those who walked under him. "It's a miracle I lived
until age 6," he says. The town's population was about thirty-
two thousand when he lived there, he recalls, "and in a town

like that you walk everywhere when you're a child. . . . A lot of things, we didn't have; we were a poor family. So you start with basics, and you respect them." The family did not own a car until he was twelve, or a telephone until he was fifteen, after the family left Illinois.

Ray remembers being taken by his mother to see Lon Chaney's *The Hunchback of Notre Dame* when he was about three years old. When he was five, he saw the the dinosaurs of *The Lost World*, and for Christmas that year, his Aunt Neva gave him a book of fairy tales, *Once upon a Time*, which introduced him to the world of fantasy.

He tends to remember the milestones of his childhood not as his first bicycle ride or Little League home run, but as first encounters with rich lodes of literary raw material: L. Frank Baum's Oz books when he was six, science fiction magazines when he was eight (he was elated to discover the new magazine *Amazing Stories*), Tarzan the following year. In 1928 he was sick for three months with whooping cough; his mother's candlelit hours with him, reading aloud the works of Edgar Allan Poe, are echoed in the scene in *Fahrenheit 451* when Montag reads to Millie. Blackstone the Magician fascinated him when he was eleven, Jules Verne at twelve. "*King Kong* in 1933 when I was 13, H.G. Wells, . . . all those things," he recalls. His family encouraged him to read Bulfinch's *Mythology*, and Greek, Roman, and Norse myths showed him the wonders of metaphor. "My childhood was packed with metaphors. Plus the Bible. Plus the hundreds of other films during that time."

By the age of nine or ten, he was dizzy with delight at the wealth available at the public library, spending at least two nights a week indulging himself there. In a 1994 National Public Radio interview, he talked about what libraries had meant to him:

> The early days of your life, when we're all 10, 11, 12, those are the greatest days in the history of your living, aren't they? When you love books so completely, you vanish into them, you become part of them. You can't even be called out for supper. And your parents can't get you out of the book. We never have that experience quite the same way when we're older. We still love books, but we're not immersed, drowning, in them. So with that background, and needing the libraries as part of my life, as my university, they came to occupy the center of my life.

Not just an avid reader, "I was really quite a glutton" for books, he recalls. "I used to memorize entire books. I suppose that's where the ending of *Fahrenheit 451* comes from—where the book people wander through the wilderness and each of them is a book. That was me when I was ten. I was *Tarzan of the Apes*."

THE SHADOW SIDE

> Bradbury's strength lies in the fact that he writes about the things that are really important to us—not the things we pretend we are interested in—science, marriage, sports, politics, crime—but the fundamental prerational fears and longings and desires: the rage at being born; the will to be loved; the longing to communicate; the hatred of parents and siblings, the fear of things that are not self.

With these words Damon Knight hit on one of Bradbury's most seductive and powerful traits: he is not afraid to confront and portray his darkest feelings.

For example, Ray's first close experience with death came when his grandfather died in 1926. That same year, his parents had their last child, a daughter, Elizabeth. Fifty years later, Bradbury told interviewer Robert Jacobs,

> We all have lists of people we would like to kill, starting when we were children, when the first competition comes into the family. When I was six and my sister was born, I was displaced and wished her dead. The next thing I knew, she was. She died of pneumonia when I was seven. . . . For a little while you say, "Hey, wow! She's gone!" Then you suddenly remember that she's not coming back *ever*, and it hurts and you have mixed feelings of sorrow and guilt. . . . The purpose, then, of a *good* horror story is to exorcise these demons; is to bring them out and say, "Look, you're no different than anyone else."

Ray also suffered from being the unathletic, "four-eyed" boy with glasses. He remembers being the butt of practical jokes, being pushed around and taunted. As he told Jacobs,

> I saw reality very clear when I was very young; 10, 11, 12 years old. I didn't care for the male animal. We're not a very nice sex. Men and boys are real destroyers, and I didn't like growing up in a destructive environment where I had the hell beat out of me all the time. I wasn't very good at fighting and I wasn't very good at running and I didn't like it! Being a boy from, say, the age of 11 to 15 is *really* hell on wheels! . . . So I pulled away and formed my own world: Ray Bradbury, Incorporated! I stuck up my finger at them and I said, "Screw all of you! I'm going my way. I'm quitting this part of the human race until I get big enough so you'll all have to come back and tip your hats!"

When his fourth-grade friends made fun of his beloved collection of Buck Rogers comic strips, he tore them up—

then mourned for a month. Finally he decided, "Those are not my friends, the ones who got me to tear the strips apart and so tear my own life down the middle; those are my enemies." He started collecting Buck Rogers again—and Flash Gordon, and Prince Valiant—and says, "My life has been happy ever since. For that was the beginning of my writing science fiction. Since then, I have never listened to anyone who criticized my taste in space-travel, sideshows or gorillas. When such occurs, I pack up my dinosaurs and leave the room."

Ray learned to go his own way, but he did not forget his unhappy experiences, reflected in his writing, for example, when Captain Beatty says this to Montag in *Fahrenheit 451:*

> With school turning out more runners, jumpers, racers, tinkerers, grabbers, snatchers, fliers, and swimmers instead of examiners, critics, knowers, and imaginative creators, the word "intellectual," of course, became the swear word it deserved to be. . . . Surely you remember the boy in your own school class who was exceptionally bright. . . . And wasn't it this bright boy you selected for beatings and tortures after hours? Of course it was.

Leaving Waukegan

Leonard Bradbury moved his family to Tucson, Arizona, in October 1926, shortly after Ray started first grade, then moved back to Waukegan the following May. They remained in Illinois until 1932, when Leonard was laid off from his job in the middle of the depression. Hoping to find employment, the Bradburys moved to Tucson again. Although they were only in Arizona for a year or so this time, it was a pivotal period for Ray. For one thing, he got a job. "I loved radio and went and hung around the local station there in Tucson [KGAR] and told my friends I was getting a job as a radio announcer," he told the *Tucson Weekly*'s Jim Nintzel. He would race to the station after school and get underfoot until he finally was given a spot: reading comic strips to kids on Saturday. It was a perfect occupation for someone who had been collecting comics since he was nine, he remembers, and it paid exceedingly well: "My pay was free tickets to see *King Kong, Murders in the Wax Museum* and *The Mummy.* You can't do any better than that. I've never had better income in my life since." Ray believes that his fascination with comic strips has helped him both in prose and scriptwriting, since he studied and learned from the way the cartoon artists put together their storyboards.

He was already writing stories—on rolls of butcher paper since the previous year—but this Christmas in Tucson, his parents gave him a six-dollar toy dial typewriter, which he used to write his own Buck Rogers stories, as well as a sequel to Edgar Rice Burroughs's *John Carter of Mars* (he was too impatient to wait a year for the next installment). Many of his stories were on the weird side: "From the time I was 12 until I was 22 or 23, I wrote stories long after midnight—unconventional stories of ghosts and haunts and things in jars that I had seen in sour armpit carnivals, of friends lost to the tides in lakes, and of consorts of three in the morning, those souls who had to fly in the dark in order not to be shot in the sun."

His other pursuits were less eerie. He sang the lead in the school operetta, indulging a desire to perform that had already found expression in his efforts to become the world's best stage magician (he had sent off to Chicago for some magic tricks, and performed them for the Waukegan Oddfellows and the American Legion). He listened to the nighttime radio serial *Chandu the Magician* and each night, after the show, wrote out the script from memory.

LOS ANGELES AND HOLLYWOOD

In May 1933, Ray's father quit his Tucson job (selling "chili bricks" to restaurants) and moved the family back to Waukegan for the last time. That summer, Ray and his Aunt Neva attended the Chicago World's Fair, where he was enthralled by the City of the Future in the Century of Progress exhibit.

Work was still difficult to find in Illinois, though, and after Ray's Uncle Einar moved to California in January 1934, Leonard Bradbury decided to try his luck there too. In April, the family moved to Los Angeles with only forty dollars to pay rent and buy food until Leonard could find work. Fortunately, he soon found both a steady job (making wire at a cable company for fourteen dollars a week) and an apartment in the middle of Hollywood. Ray was ecstatic. He rollerskated to movie studios, premieres, and popular hangouts, badgering movie stars for autographs so engagingly that he was rewarded with amused tolerance. Comedians George Burns and Gracie Allen, for example, let Ray and a friend be an audience of two as they aired their new radio show. Every week, Ray wrote a skit or vignette for the show, and every week George Burns thanked him politely, until one week he actually used an eight-line bit to end the show.

Ray found out that the girl who lived next door had a real typewriter, and was willing to type out his stories as he dictated them—*much* faster than his toy dial typewriter. (He would buy his own first real typewriter in 1937 for ten dollars, using cash saved from his lunch money.) Now that he could produce typed manuscripts, he began submitting his work to major magazines, such as the *Saturday Evening Post,* without success.

In 1935 he entered Los Angeles High School. During his years there he was active in the poetry club and the drama club (he decided to become an actor, as well as a magician, cartoonist, architect, and many other professions, nearly all of which goals were realized over the years). He took a short-story class and a poetry class (his poem "In Memory to Will Rogers" was his first published item, appearing in the *Waukegan News-Sun* on August 16, 1936); wrote the script for the school's annual talent show in 1937, for which he also served as assistant producer/director; and played the lead in a one-act play. In later years he told composer and music journalist Mark Gresham that he had begun to write poetry when he was about fifteen, when he found and read some old copies of *Coronet* magazine with pictures by such top photographers as Alfred Steiglitz. "I got into poetry, in a way, by tying myself to an image," he said. He later noted that when he wrote the poems to go with the photographs, "it was a metaphor on top of a metaphor."

In October 1937 he discovered others who shared his love of science fiction and joined the Los Angeles Science Fiction League, a group of enthusiasts who met at Clinton's Cafeteria. Within a few months he was contributing articles, cartoons, and columns to several fan publications (fanzines), making contacts with famous pros such as Robert Heinlein and Henry Kuttner and gathering knowledge that would eventually help him sell stories to the magazines he had long loved reading.

INTO THE ADULT WORLD

Ray graduated in June 1938, wearing his uncle's jacket; his uncle had been slain wearing it, and it still bore the bullet holes. As he recalled in an interview with Jeffrey Elliot in the late 1970s, "When I left high school, we were very poor. In fact, we were on relief when I graduated. We had few prospects for the future. It was 1938, and there were nearly fifteen million people unemployed." He immediately began selling newspapers on L.A. street corners for ten dollars a week, but he continued his education, not by going to college—that was out of the question—but by going to libraries, by forming a study group with friends that met nightly, by joining a little theater group and writing plays as well as acting, by taking a night course in the short story at L.A. High, by studying science fiction writing with Robert Heinlein. He continued to read voraciously, as he recalled in a 1997 interview with *People Online:*

> Steinbeck and Hemingway, John Collier, a wonderful short-story writer who did a lot of scripts for Alfred Hitchcock's TV series and *The Twilight Zone.* Writers like Willa Cather, a lot of women writers. Edith Wharton. Eudora Welty. I read every short story by every American writer over the years going back to Washington Irving, Poe, Melville. Rudyard Kipling and Dickens in England. I pretty well educated myself in the short story in every country in the world. If you're going to write them, you better know them.

He published four issues of a fanzine called *Futuria Fantasia,* thus self-publishing his first stories in magazines that also contained work by his friends Kuttner, Heinlein, and others. *Futuria Fantasia* received financial backing from Forrest Ackerman, whom he later described as "editor, publisher, and backer" who "kept my spirits up during my 18th, 19th and 20th years while I wrote my pretty terrible short stories and sent them off to be rejected." He was gathering plenty of rejections, since he was writing one thousand words of fiction every day—and selling nothing.

Ackerman lent him the fare to New York for the first World Science Fiction Fair, or Nycon, at the beginning of July. While he was there, he served as artist's representative for his artist friend Hannes Bok, now a well-known illustrator (Bok's art had graced the covers of *Futuria Fantasia;* thanks to Ray's efforts, *Weird Tales* used some of his work) and went to the New York World's Fair. Little did he know that the next time the World's Fair would come to New York, in 1964, he would be commissioned to write *An American Journey,* a film history of the country, for the U.S. government pavilion.

Back in L.A., Ray continued reading and writing, and selling newspapers on the corner. He rented a tiny "office" in a tenement building, where he installed his typewriter and followed Kuttner's advice: "Ray, stop running around bothering people with your ideas. Stop tearing at every sleeve you can find and shouting in people's ears about your grand ideas. Go home, get your typewriter out, and *write!* You can't *say* you want to be a writer, you have to *write* to be a writer!" He read Dorothea Brande's 1934 book, *Becoming a Writer*, which suggested free-association techniques to access the power of the subconscious. With the help of Robert and Leslyn Heinlein, who held a weekly science fiction writing class, one of his pieces was placed in the West Coast magazine *Script*, another nonpaying market. He also spent time with Julius Schwartz, who would soon become his agent.

Finally, in 1941, he made his first sale. He and fellow writer Henry Hasse collaborated on "Pendulum," for which *Super Science Stories* paid $27.50. The magazine appeared on the newsstands just in time for his twenty-first birthday.

Of the fifty-two short stories he wrote that year, he sold three. As he wrote in "Drunk, and in Charge of a Bicycle," his introduction to the 1983 collection *The Stories of Ray Bradbury*, "For ten years I wrote at least one short story a week, somehow guessing that a day would finally come when I truly got out of the way and let it happen." He was right; it happened at last the following year:

> The day came in 1942 when I wrote "The Lake." Ten years of doing everything wrong suddenly became the right idea, the right scene, the right characters, the right day, the right creative time. I wrote the story sitting outside, with my typewriter, on the lawn. At the end of an hour the story was finished, the hair on the back of my neck was standing up, and I was in tears. I knew I had written the first really good story of my life.

OCCUPATION: WRITER

Although "The Lake" would not be published for a couple of years, Bradbury had finally found his voice, and gradually found a market. He sold a half-dozen stories in 1942 (his friend Henry Kuttner wrote the ending to his first story for *Weird Tales*, "The Candle," hammering out a quick couple hundred words to replace his "clumsy" and "conventional" ending) and twice that many in 1943, when he finally gave up selling newspapers and committed himself to the profession of writing. (When asked in later years to provide author information for the Book-of-the-Month-Club, he wrote under *Profession:* "Newsboy, Los Angeles, California, 1940–43; full-time writer, 1943–"). It was hardly a lucrative practice at this point: "There was another reason to write so much: I was being paid twenty to forty dollars a story, by the pulp magazines. High on the hog was hardly my way of life. I had to sell at least one story, or better two, each month in order to survive my hot-dog, hamburger, trolley-car-fare life."

He was writing in genres other than science fiction; at the time most editors were looking for certain formulaic science fiction that was not his style. He decided to try his hand at mysteries, and by 1944 he had stories accepted by several pulp mystery magazines, including *Flynn's Detective Fiction, Detective Tales, Dime Mystery,* and *New Detective.* In the meantime, although his eyesight had kept him out of the army (the United States had entered World War II after the bombing of Pearl Harbor in December 1941), he was also making his own contribution to the war effort, writing radio material for the Red Cross and scripts for the Los Angeles Department of Civil Defense. His friend Leigh Brackett, another writer who had been helping him learn to write and whose style he admired and tried to imitate, asked him to help her out: she was busy writing a screenplay and facing a deadline for her half-finished space-opera novella, "Lorelei of the Red Mist." He finished the book for her, so successfully that "people cannot tell when they read that story where she leaves off and where I begin. I have trouble finding the exact spot myself," as he told writer David Mogen.

Although he was beginning to be successful, he was still far from where he wanted to be, and becoming impatient. He told Charles Platt, author of *Dream Makers: Science Fiction and Fantasy Writers at Work* that when he was about twenty-four, trying to sell stories to the "slicks"—*Colliers, Harper's,* The *Atlantic Monthly*—and hoping his stories would be chosen for the *Best American Short Stories* anthologies, he asked to "borrow" a friend's psychiatrist for an afternoon. For the princely fee of twenty dollars an hour ("That was my salary for the whole week to go to this guy for an hour"), he went to the psychiatrist and complained, "Nothing's happening." When the doctor asked what he wanted to happen, he responded, "I want to be the greatest writer that ever lived." The doctor suggested that might take a little time, and told him, "Go down to the library and read the lives of Balzac and Du Maupassant and Dickens and Tolstoy, and see how long it took them to become what they became." Bradbury took the advice:

> I went and read and discovered that they had to wait, too. And a year later I began to sell to the *American Mercury,* and *Colliers,* and I appeared in *The Best American Short Stories* when I was twenty-six. I still wasn't making any money, but I was getting recognition I wanted, the love that I wanted from people I looked up to. The intellectual elite in America was beginning to say, "Hey, you're okay, you're all right, and you're

going to make it." And then my girlfriend Maggie told me the same thing. And then it didn't matter whether the people around me sneered at me. I was willing to wait.

MAGGIE

In a brief article in its issue of April 4, 1994, *Publishers Weekly* reported the expected closing of two Los Angeles–area bookstores. One was a twenty-six-year-old Laguna Beach bookstore called Fahrenheit 451, suffering from a bookkeeper's embezzlement. The second was the venerable Fowler Brothers, an independent bookstore and stationery shop that was facing bankruptcy after more than a century in downtown Los Angeles. *PW* noted, "Science fiction writer Ray Bradbury met his future wife, a Fowler's salesclerk, at the store when she mistook him for a shoplifter close to 50 years ago." Apparently her first impression improved fairly readily; she agreed to go out for coffee.

Ray remembered what dating in those lean years was like: "I couldn't take girls out and give them a halfway decent evening. I could give them a ten-cent malted milk and a cheap movie, and then walk them home. We couldn't take the bus, there was no money left."

Maggie—Marguerite Susan McClure—was the only woman he ever dated. She was obviously not after Ray for his money: "Her views were so much like mine—she was interested in books, in language, in literature—and she *wasn't* interested in having a rich boyfriend; which was great, because I wasn't!" One of their favorite dates was to go to the beach, where Maggie would read poetry aloud; Ray later translated these dates into such short stories as "And the Moon Be Still as Bright" and "There Will Come Soft Rains."

Ray and Maggie were married in 1947 and moved to a small apartment in Venice, California. That same year August Derleth's Arkham House published Bradbury's first book, *Dark Carnival,* a collection of twenty-seven terrifying stories. Arkham House notes that "eight years after the book's publication, Bradbury allowed fifteen of the *Dark Carnival* tales to be reprinted in a volume called *The October Country*—but only after he had edited and rewritten some of them, downplaying the more horrific elements for the mass audience he had by then attracted." Unfortunately, it had taken all of those eight years for the three-thousand-book printing to sell out. (Today, of course, books from that printing are extremely rare and can be valuable.)

Money was still tight, but as Ray reported three decades later, "In thirty-two years of marriage we have had only one problem with money. One incident, with a play. The rest of the time we never discussed it. We knew we didn't have any money in the bank, so why discuss something you don't have?"

However, adding children to the money equation "terrified us," he remembered. He had sold many stories, but was hoping for book publication that would be more lucrative than the Arkham House project. Maggie was pregnant with their first child in 1949 when friend and fellow author Norman Corwin urged Bradbury to go to New York to meet with book editors in person. He and Maggie scraped together enough money for a one-way ticket for the four-day bus trip; Ray stayed in a YMCA dorm for five dollars a week.

Doubleday editor William Bradbury (no relation to Ray) took him to lunch at Luchow's and suggested he try working his stories about Mars into a novel. Returning to the YMCA, he arranged the stories into a sequence and realized he only needed to write short "interchapters" to link them into a coherent whole. The next day Doubleday accepted the outline for *The Martian Chronicles,* and gave Ray a fifteen-hundred-dollar advance for two novels.

He was halfway home on the bus before he realized he could have afforded to take the train, even the Pullman sleeper, all the way to Los Angeles. (He did not fly until he was in his sixties; as he writes in *Fahrenheit 451,* "Do you know the legend of Hercules and Antaeus, the giant wrestler, whose strength was incredible so long as he stood firmly on the earth? But when he was held, rootless, in midair, by Hercules, he perished easily. If there isn't something in that legend for us today, in this city, in our time, then I am completely insane.")

Thus, by the time their first daughter, Susan Marguerite, arrived in 1949, "God began to provide," as Ray put it, and his income nearly doubled to ninety dollars a week. This still did not allow for splurges such as for furniture, for example. When *The Martian Chronicles* came out in 1950, Ray held a book signing at a Santa Monica bookstore. He recognized the novelist Christopher Isherwood when he walked into the store, and Ray offered him a copy of the new book. Ray inscribed the book to Isherwood, but never expected to see him again. A few days later, a friend called to tell him that Isherwood wanted to visit Bradbury. "If he does, he'll have to sit on the floor," Ray said. "Marguerite and I don't have any furniture in the living room yet."

DISCOVERY

Isherwood had just been named book reviewer for *Tomorrow* magazine, and had decided that *The Martian Chronicles* would be the first book he would review. As James Gunn writes in *The Road to Science Fiction*, "Isherwood 'discovered' Bradbury in the science fiction ghetto and announced his genius to the world." As Brian Aldiss puts it in his history of science fiction, *Billion Year Spree*, "His name became famous overnight, and he has remained one of our eminent dreamers ever since."

Isherwood also introduced Bradbury to other celebrated and influential writers, including Aldous Huxley, who had moved to Los Angeles from England, and Zen writer Gerald Heard, both of whom widely praised Ray's work. He was now considered in the same league as such writers as Isaac Asimov, Arthur C. Clarke, and his old friend and teacher, Robert Heinlein. He did not want to be considered "just" a science fiction author, though, and with his next book, *The Illustrated Man*, he extended his reputation as a popular writer.

In 1951 the television series *Tales of Tomorrow* used a couple of his stories; thanks to his "cartoon" days, much of his writing translates easily to storyboard-driven TV and movie scripts. The following year Universal Studios asked him to write a story in which Something comes from Outer Space. He realized the producers had in mind a kind of story he thought would be vulgar and obvious, so he made a deal; he would write two story treatments, one their way and one the way he envisioned it. If they liked his version, he would produce a fuller version; if they preferred the one they had asked for, no hard feelings, but he would not keep working on it. To his amazement, they loved his version of *It Came from Outer Space* (although they did not follow his advice to keep the monster in the dark and thereby avoid turning the movie into a comedy by revealing its Hollywood monster appearance). He was so excited that he provided practically an entire screenplay, even though he was only to be paid for a much shorter treatment. He received a happier payoff some years later, though, when director Steven Spielberg shook his hand after Ray previewed *Close Encounters of the Third Kind*. "How did you like *your* film?" asked Spielberg, explaining that *Close Encounters* would never have been made if he had not seen *It Came from Outer Space* a half-dozen times when he was a child.

FAHRENHEIT 451: A PROTEST

During this period, the House Un-American Activities Committee and Senator Joseph McCarthy were engaged in trying to expose and destroy what they considered subversive elements in the United States. Using broad attacks, innuendo, and guilt by association, they had made Hollywood one of their major targets, convinced it was a hotbed of communist sympathizers and saboteurs. Ray was not wildly political, but he was one of the few members of the Screen Writers Guild who objected to the loyalty oath the group required to protect itself against communists. Nonetheless, Hollywood was his home, and the people being persecuted were his coworkers. In 1950 he wrote the short story "The Fireman," which he would later expand into *Fahrenheit 451.*

Many events and situations fed into the creation of the novel. For example, one night he was walking with a friend in Los Angeles (he has never learned to drive), when a policeman stopped them at the corner of Wilshire and Western. As he told a National Public Radio interviewer, when the officer asked what they were doing, Ray responded, "Putting one foot in front of the other." And when the policeman did not like that answer, Ray went on, "It doesn't make any sense logically that we would call attention to ourselves by walking. . . . If we were criminals, we would drive up in a car, burgle the joint, and drive away. That's the way you do things in our society." The policeman did not appreciate his logic, and after an angry argument, Ray went home and wrote a short story, "The Pedestrian," about a society that has outlawed walking. Then, a month or two later,

> Out of that short story, I took my pedestrian out for a walk, he turned a corner and there's a little young girl standing in the middle of the sidewalk and she looks at him and she sniffs his uniform. She says, "You smell of kerosene. I know who you are. You're Montag, the fireman, the man who burns books." And nine days later the novel was finished.

By then there were two children at home (Ramone Anne was born in May 1951) and Ray, who has always been a child at heart, confessed he found them distracting: "I worked in the garage, but the girls would come out and tap on the window and ask me to come out and play. And, of course, Daddy would, and that means our income went out the window."

Searching for a quiet place to write, he heard typewriter-tapping in the basement of the UCLA library. "I went downstairs and . . . here's a typing room where for 10 cents a half hour you could rent a typewriter. And I thought, my gosh, this is terrific, I can be here a couple hours a day, it'll cost me thirty, forty cents, and get my work done. So . . . I got the idea for *Fahrenheit 451* and I got $9.50 worth of dimes and spent the next nine days writing the novel."

CONQUERING OTHER REALMS

The children were not always a distraction; sometimes they sparked an idea for a story. A couple of weeks after Susan, their first daughter, was born, she woke up in the night crying, but she was neither hungry, wet, nor stuck by a diaper pin. Remembering his own birth, Ray turned to Maggie and said, "I remember something like this. You know what she's going through? . . . She's having a nightmare. It's obvious!" Maggie was doubtful: "What can she have a nightmare about? She's only two weeks old." But Ray was convinced she remembered the trauma of being born, as he had, so he wrote a book for her, *Switch on the Night*. It would be published a few years later, in 1955, the year the Bradburys' third daughter, Bettina Francion, was born.

Other writing opportunities presented themselves. Bradbury was asked by director John Huston to write the screenplay for *Moby Dick*. He and Maggie packed up the kids and sailed to Ireland to live from October 1953 to April 1954 while he wrote about the great whale. He describes the serendipity of that assignment: "I was greatly influenced by the great poets, by Shakespeare, my love of dinosaurs starting when I was 6. The combination caused me to write 'The Fog Horn,' [about] a dinosaur falling in love with a lighthouse. When John Huston read that story, he thought I'd been influenced by Melville. But it was Shakespeare. That's how I got the job writing the screenplay for *Moby Dick*." While he was working on that project he was also absorbing new material that would eventually be used in *The Anthem Sprinters* and *Green Shadows, White Whale*.

Just as "The Fog Horn" had led to *Moby Dick*, that project led to others: "Because of *Moby Dick*," he wrote in "Drunk, and in Charge of a Bicycle,"

> I reexamined the life of Melville and Jules Verne, compared their mad captains in an essay written to reintroduce a new translation of *20,000 Leagues Beneath the Sea*, which, read by

the 1964 New York World's Fair people, put me in charge of conceptualizing the entire upper floor of the United States Pavilion.

Because of the Pavilion, the Disney organization hired me to help plan the dreams that went into Spaceship Earth, part of Epcot, a permanent world's fair.

His vision has been tapped by city planners and business-people; when asked to help revive a moribund downtown San Diego, he helped design the whimsical and visually stimulating Horton Plaza shopping center, and the Glendale Galleria, built to revive downtown Glendale, was based on his concept. He has ambitious ideas for turning Los Angeles into eighty or so friendly, unique neighborhoods, where people will walk and gather and a vibrant community will form. As Leon Worden reported in 1995,

Bradbury still pursues his dreams, routinely advising archi-tectural designers and urban planners across the continent on ways to make their endeavors appealing to potential tourists and shoppers. Last week he was in New Orleans, talking to 800 mall producers. The week before, he was keynote speaker at the Antelope Valley business conference.

This self-described "master of the obvious" applies to the here-and-now his uncanny ability to see things for what they are, and as they could be.

In *Yestermorrow*, subtitled "Obvious Answers to Impossi-ble Futures" and dedicated to Walt Disney, Bradbury dis-cusses how he has sat in "with groups, sometimes with mu-seums, sometimes with corporations, to tell them who they are . . . (to) find their metaphor."

Then there are Bradbury's ideas that others have run with: Scientists and engineers working on virtual reality machines call him "the father of virtual reality," he reports, because of his short story "The Veldt" (which carries the wall-screens of *Fahrenheit 451* into a new dimension), and, he says, "When a bright Sony inventor read about my seashell radios [in *Fahrenheit 451*], he invented the Walkman."

On the other hand, this visionary who thinks we should have colonized Mars by now has no use for such modern contrivances as the Internet. "I don't understand this whole thing about computers and the superhighway. Who wants to be in touch with all of those people?" he asked an inter-viewer. And while he is delighted that *The Martian Chroni-cles* has been made into a CD-ROM game, believing that for-mat is a logical next step, he has no interest in playing it.

His old delight in the theater reasserts itself every few

years, when he feels called upon to stage one of his plays. He says to Maggie, "Shall we open the window and throw money out again?" for they both know that his theatrical endeavors are usually costly fun, but as he says, "Working as your own producer, all the fun that *should* be in the theater comes to the surface. I have rarely had such a glorious time in my life."

Although in 1955 he failed to come up with a satisfactory adaptation of *Fahrenheit 451* when he tried to turn it into a play for Charles Laughton, in 1997 there was a brief and relatively unheralded run in New York of *Fahrenheit 451—the Musical.* Other musical endeavors have been better received; for example, he wrote the lyrics to the cantata *Christus Apollo,* which Charlton Heston narrated when it was performed in Los Angeles in 1969.

Since he wrote his Mars stories, he has often been called on to comment on humanity's attempt to explore space. In 1967, *Life* magazine sent him on assignment to the Manned Spacecraft Center in Houston, which felt like "coming home" to the boy who had dreamed of space flight since he was nine years old. His report of what he found in Houston, "An Impatient Gulliver Above Our Roots," is a paean to his fellow dreamers (especially astronauts), an awestruck, romantic view of the facility, and an excited "I told you so" to those who laughed at him when he spoke of traveling through space and colonizing other planets.

Naturally, when the unmanned space probe *Pathfinder* landed on Mars, he was the first person many newspeople called for comment. He was excited, but felt the landing was long overdue. On the other hand, when microscopic worm shells were found on the underside of a rust-colored meteorite from Mars in 1996, and some scientists immediately proclaimed this as proof there had been (and might still be) life on the red planet, his response surprised some of those who called, including reporter David Colton:

> "Here we go. I suppose this is about Mars again," snarled Ray Bradbury. . . .
>
> "I hope it's true with all my heart, but this is nonsense. There's just no proof," Bradbury said. "Ted Koppel called last night and asked me to be on 'Nightline,' but I refused because I didn't want to be a grouch.
>
> "We are here, dead matter left on Earth and struck by lightning and somehow life developed. We are something that is totally impossible," Bradbury said. . . . "It's time we land on Mars to find out for ourselves. Then there will be life on Mars and that life will be us."

All his other interests notwithstanding, Bradbury has never abandoned his belief in speculative writing. "Science fiction," he has said, "is the most important literature in the history of the world, because it's the history of ideas, the history of our civilization birthing itself. . . . Science fiction is central to everything we've ever done, and people who make fun of science fiction writers don't know what they're talking about." He believes it is vital to our progress, too: "Science fiction is the history of towns and cities yet unbuilt, ghosting our imaginations and lifting us to rise up and find hammers and nails to build our dreams before they blow away."

But, ever unconventional, he has his own definition of himself: "I am not so much a science fiction writer (which many deny) as I am an Idea Beast. Any idea that nags or bites or waves at me I respond to with a yell and a dash for the typewriter."

He never suffers from writer's block. As he told *People Online* in 1997, "I awake every morning at 7 and lie in bed with collections of metaphors swimming around in my head. When they reach a peak and characters are talking to each other I then leap up and go to the typewriter and write the story. It all has to do with my subconscious, my muse. . . . It's blind driving and it's fun. This has been my process for 40 to 45 years."

He frequently gives lectures on writing to would-be authors, hoping to share his passion and enthusiasm—and warning that those without such passion should not be writers. Asked about immortality, he points to his four daughters (the fourth, Alexandra Allison, was born in 1958) and his grandchildren, and says that is all the immortality he requires. The idea of death "provokes you into creativity," he says. "The sense of death has been with me always. It's a wall there and you bounce life off of it. And you create because there is the threat of extinction, so every new book is a triumph over darkness."

He has no plans to retire; he says he will continue writing "at least until I'm 99"—and then, "God can hit me with a baseball bat."

Characters and Plot

The Characters

Guy Montag: The protagonist of the novel, Montag is a fireman—a government employee whose job it is to burn books. Montag enjoys starting fires, and at the beginning of the novel he is apparently satisfied with his role in helping the state suppress knowledge as a means of preventing social unrest. However, Montag soon realizes how unhappy he is and begins to find solace in his own hidden cache of books, which he has collected over his years as a fireman. As he reads, his views of society begin to change and he finds himself at odds with his fellow firemen and the law. Ultimately Montag becomes a hunted man and escapes from the city to a colony of men who understand the value of intellectual freedom.

Mildred Montag (Mille): Montag's wife is an unhappy woman, as evidenced by her overdose on tranquilizers at the beginning of the novel, her manic drives around town in her car, and her obsession with any distraction from her own life. She watches countless hours of television and has withdrawn into her own world of labor-saving machines and simplistic entertainment. When Guy reveals his cache of books to her, she is frightened and encourages him to get rid of them. Eventually, she betrays her husband by having his library burned. She flees their marriage, and at the end of the novel Montag speculates that she is obliviously watching TV as the blast levels the futuristic city.

Clarisse McClellan: Montag's new neighbor, the sixteen-year-old Clarisse, appears in only a few scenes at the beginning of the novel. However, Montag's few meetings with the girl awaken his unease with his role as a fireman; her curiosity and enjoyment of life make him realize how unhappy he has become. She is killed early in the novel by a hit-and-run driver, symbolizing the fate of nonconformists in an uncaring, repressive, sadistic society.

Unnamed Woman: After a neighbor tells the firemen about an old woman's library, Montag's company of firemen come to burn her books. She chooses to die with her books, and her self-sacrifice makes Montag wonder what power books could contain that is worth dying for.

Captain Beatty: The cynical leader of the firemen is actually a well-read man who privately respects Montag's interest in books. However, while Captain Beatty knows that books offer other—perhaps better—ways of constructing a society, he realizes that admitting this would make his life meaningless, and thus he continues to view books as an enemy. Beatty wants Montag to agree that book burning is for the good of society. When Beatty discovers Montag's hidden library, he asks Montag to set the fire: Montag instead turns the flamethrower on his captain. As Beatty is burned, he offers no resistance, suggesting that he is tired of living in an unhappy, oppressive world.

Professor Faber: With his graying hair and brittle bones, Faber, a retired English professor, acts as a grandfatherly mentor to Montag, who seeks out Faber to learn more about books. Faber places great importance on individual life and freedom, but is pessimistic and embittered about his society's condemnation of these values. He discusses books and philosophy with Montag, but also emphasizes his own cowardice regarding his conformity. Yet Faber also helps Montag in his confrontation with Beatty, and provides Guy with the means to successfully escape the city.

The Mechanical Hound: The Mechanical Hound is an eight-legged glass and metal contraption that serves as a surveillance tool and programmable killing machine for the firemen, who use it to track down suspected book hoarders and readers. Montag suspects the Hound somehow knows about his secret collection of books, and in his escape from the city it is the deadly Hound, a symbol of the ruthless, efficient state, that he must evade.

Granger: Granger is the leader of a group of outcasts known collectively as "the book people," who have all memorized and thus "become" a book in order to preserve literature. First Granger helps Montag throw the Hound off his trail, then he welcomes Montag into the book people's commune and its spiritual appreciation of books. In contrast to the hostile, oppressive city, Granger and his commune represent intellectualism and enlightenment, and the fulfillment of Montag's quest.

THE PLOT

The novel opens with "fireman" Guy Montag exulting in his job of burning books: "It was a pleasure to burn." In his futuristic society, where houses are built to be fireproof and firemen are no longer needed as firefighters, almost all books (with the exception of a few manuals and other material considered necessary) are outlawed. Firemen burn books, along with the interiors of the homes of the people who illegally possess them.

Firemen work at night, since the spectacle of burning—intended to be both lesson and entertainment for the citizenry—makes a more impressive show in the dark. Thus it is still dark as he is going home from work. Walking along the sidewalk near his house, he meets Clarisse, a young girl who demonstrates an extraordinary characteristic in this totalitarian state: tireless curiosity. She takes the time to stop and observe; as she observes Montag, he sees himself in her eyes, not the fireman who frightens most people, but "just a man, after all."

Her gentle questions—"Is it true that long ago firemen put fires *out* . . . ?" "Why are you laughing?" "Are you happy?"—and pointed observations—"You never stop to think . . ."; "I sometimes think drivers don't know what grass is, or flowers, because they never see them slowly"—make him uneasy, but he finds that she, and the questions she has raised, remain on his mind as he enters his home. Her face is like a mirror, he decides, unlike the faces of other people, which he compares to torches that burn out, never reflecting back on those around them.

He goes into his bedroom, expecting to find his wife, Mildred, asleep with little thimble radios called Seashells tamped tightly into her ears. She is asleep, but she has taken too many sleeping pills. As he turns to call the emergency hospital, jet bombers scream overhead.

In response to his call, two technicians arrive to pump out Mildred's stomach and replace all the blood in her body; she is just one of the many such cases the handymen treat every night, and they leave after briskly demanding payment for their service. As Montag watches his sleeping wife, her color fresh with the replacement blood, he finds himself wishing they could also have replaced her brain, her memory, her flesh.

Opening the windows, he hears the conversation and quiet, unforced laughter of Clarisse and her family across the lawn. An unnamed yearning draws him into their yard, where he eavesdrops on their conversation, a rueful discussion of how people have become interchangeable and disposable. He returns home and goes to bed, tearfully realizing that the world in which he was once so self-assured, so pleased with his position in it, has changed: "I don't know anything any more."

The next morning, Mildred is hungry, as the emergency technicians had warned she would be, but she has no memory and little curiosity about what happened the night before. Later, when he tells her she had taken an entire bottle of thirty sleeping pills, she denies that she would do such a thing, then returns to studying a script.

She explains to Montag that she will have a part in the wall-to-wall circuit television program that comes on in a few minutes. By mailing in boxtops, she has bought the right to play the homemaker in the play; every few minutes, the characters on the screens on all three walls of the TV parlor will turn toward her and ask for her "opinion." Her character, "Helen," then responds with scripted answers: "I think that's fine!" When Montag asks what the play is about, she tells him it's about "these people named Bob and Ruth and Helen," and urges him to consider buying an expensive fourth wall for the TV parlor so it will seem "like this room wasn't ours at all, but all kinds of exotic people's rooms."

As he leaves for work, he meets Clarisse again, walking in the rain and holding the last of the season's dandelion flowers. She rubs it under her chin, telling him that the yellow that rubs off means she's in love. When she rubs it under his chin and proclaims that he is not in love with anyone, he vehemently denies the flower's evidence, but cannot conjure up the face of his beloved.

Clarisse tells him she is on her way to see a psychiatrist, required for one so out of sync with the rest of society. She says she tells the psychiatrist that "sometimes I just sit and *think*. But I won't tell them what. I've got them running." Then she tells him that he is not like other people, who walk away or threaten her when she expresses herself. The night before, when she told him that if you look, you can see a man in the moon, he had stopped and looked. She finds the fact that he puts up with her especially strange in a fireman, which makes her think that vocation is not right for him.

When he arrives at the fire station, he stops for a while to watch the Mechanical Hound sleeping. This contraption of metal, electrical circuits, and glass has been engineered to follow any programmed scent and kill its prey with an injection of drugs. During slow periods the firemen set the Hound on cats or chickens or rats, for a few seconds of fun in watching it work. Montag no longer takes part in the group game of betting which of its prey the Hound will catch first; now he stays upstairs, avoiding the bloodthirsty pastime. Yet he is fascinated by the machine. When he approaches and touches it, it wakens and growls, seemingly undecided about whether he is designated prey. Montag escapes quickly up the firepole and the beast goes back to sleep.

Montag tells his boss, Captain Beatty, that the Hound dislikes him. Beatty says that is impossible for a mechanical contraption, but Montag hypothesizes that someone may have programmed the Hound with part of his chemical combination, making it react but not attack—something that has happened to him twice before. Beatty says he will have the Hound checked for malfunctions, but Montag wonders to himself whether someone has discovered that he has hidden books in his home and "told" the Hound about his crime.

For the next few days, he sees Clarisse every time he leaves his house, and soon feels he has known her for years. She stays out of school, saying she will not be missed because she is labeled antisocial, a classification she finds odd: So-called social people are rushed quickly from one activity to another, told what to think and never asked to think for themselves, either too tired to do anything at the end of the day except go to bed or out to wreak mayhem running down people with their cars.

She says she has no friends, but this is by choice: She is afraid of children her own age, who regularly kill each other. Instead she prefers to observe and listen to people; however, she points out to Montag, "People don't talk about anything." According to her, people see the same programs, tell the same jokes, and watch abstract patterns on the musical walls and at the museums, which no longer exhibit representational artwork.

However, after a few more days, Clarisse does not appear. Montag does not realize at first that she is gone, or that he misses her; he simply feels that something is the matter.

Back at the firehouse, as jets scream overhead, Montag fears that Beatty can sense his guilt, although he is not sure exactly what he is guilty of. He asks Beatty what happened to the man whose library they had burned the week before, and

Beatty replies that he was taken, screaming, to the asylum. Montag protests that the man was not insane, but Beatty warns that anyone who tries to fool the government and the firemen is mad. Montag wonders aloud how it would feel to "have firemen burn *our* houses and *our* books," but when Beatty asks him if he has any books, he denies it.

Their conversation is interrupted by a fire alarm, and the crew rushes to the home of an elderly lady who has been denounced by a neighbor. Usually the police take away the criminals before the firemen arrive to burn their homes, but a mistake has occurred and the woman is still in her home. As they rush inside, she recites a quote: "Play the man, Master Ridley; we shall this day light such a candle, by God's grace, in England, as I trust shall never be put out."

As her precious store of books and magazines is tumbled out of the attic, Montag tucks one under his arm before dousing the rest with kerosene. The woman refuses to leave her home and, when Montag asks Beatty to force her to leave, the captain declines, saying suicide is a familiar pattern with such fanatics. Montag urges the woman to come with him, but she defiantly sets the fire herself with a kitchen match, and remains to burn with her books. Later, at the firehouse, Beatty tells Montag the source of her quote: a man burned for heresy in the sixteenth century.

That night, at home, Montag feels alienated from Mildred; he frantically asks her where they first met, but neither of them can remember—a fact that perturbs him but seems to bother her not at all. He reflects that the walls of the TV room, with their constantly present, pseudofamiliar cast of characters, are in effect a wall between him and his wife. The characters draw Mildred into their meaningless chatter; when he asks what they talk about and how the characters are connected to one another, Mildred cannot tell him. When he asks her about Clarisse, though, she remembers that she heard that the family has moved, and she thinks the girl was run over by a car and killed.

As he tries to fall asleep, he hears the Mechanical Hound sniffing outside his door.

The next morning Montag feels sick. He tries to tell Mildred about the woman they burned with her books, but she shows no interest, talking only about the programs on TV. When Montag asks how she would feel if he quit his job, Millie angrily criticizes the woman who upset him by dying, and worries that they will lose their home if Montag leaves his job.

Their argument is interrupted by the arrival of Captain Beatty, who says he expected Montag to call in sick today, after the death of the woman the night before. He has come to explain to Montag the history of their profession, expecting this knowledge will ease his distress.

Beatty tells Montag that long ago, when books appealed only to a few people, they could afford to cater to different tastes. But as the population expanded and mass media—"films and radios, magazines, books"—were everpresent, their content was increasingly tailored to appeal to the "paste pudding norm." At the same time, everything speeded up, so books became shorter, were condensed and digested, cut down eventually to no more than an entry in a dictionary. As the pace of living sped up even more, learning and even thinking became unnecessary.

At the same time, the larger population was composed of large numbers of minorities, as people defined themselves as members of one or more subgroupings and insisted that the media not portray members of their group in any controversial way. Thus magazines became "vanilla tapioca," designed to avoid offending anyone, and books—except for comic books and three-dimensional sex magazines—died out. Beatty summarizes: "There you have it, Montag. It didn't come from the Government down. There was no dictum, no declaration, no censorship, to start with, no! Technology, mass exploitation, and minority pressure carried the trick, thank God. Today, thanks to them, you can stay happy all the time, you are allowed to read comics, the good old confessions, or trade journals."

"Intellectual" became a profanity, Beatty continues, and it became necessary for everyone to be *made* equal to everyone else. Thus, when houses were finally fireproofed, the firemen were given a new job: to burn the books that threatened to make people unequal, or to make them unhappy by giving them something to judge themselves against. The firemen, he says, are the custodians of society's peace of mind.

Not only books are burned in the effort to keep people happy, he points out; when people die, they are immediately incinerated so the survivors can get on with their lives without having to bother with memorials.

Montag asks Beatty about Clarisse; Beatty responds that such odd ducks are embarrassing, and she is better off dead. Luckily, such aberrations are rare, he says; most people respond well to the absence of choice, to encouragement to forget the impending war. People should be made to feel intelligent by being stuffed with facts, he continues, rather than being bothered with such "slippery stuff" as philosophy or sociology, which only promote melancholy.

Montag should be proud, Beatty concludes, of being among those who "stand against the small tide of those who want to make everyone unhappy with conflicting theory and thought." Then he warns that all firemen get the urge to read a book at some point—he, in fact, has read several, "to know what I was about"—and the authorities do not worry about their curiosity, as long as they burn the books within twenty-four hours. If they don't, their fellow firemen will come and burn the books for them.

After this oblique warning, he asks Montag when he will return to work; he is surprised when Montag says he is not sure when he will return, and adds as he leaves that Montag will be missed if he does not show up.

When Montag tells his wife that he feels like smashing and killing things, she urges him to do what she does when she feels that way: take the car out into the country at high speed and run over animals. Montag replies that he does not want to get rid of the feeling, even though he is very unhappy. He says he may even start reading books. Millie says he will end up in jail, then turns away from "this junk" he is talking about to attend to the announcer on the television, who addresses her constantly by name (a function of a hundred-dollar converter).

Montag turns off the television sound and insists that Millie listen. He tells her that he has hidden many books in their home over the past year, pulling them out of their hiding places and piling them on the floor as he talks. He feels she has a right to know, since discovery would cost them both their home, and asks her to look at them with him to discover if the captain is right in saying that books have nothing to offer. He begs not only to look at the books but to try to save their marriage. He begins to read to her over her horrified objections. They hear the captain return but refuse to answer the door; later, they hear the Mechanical Hound sniffing around outside.

After hours of reading, Millie tries to explain that "books aren't people. You read and I look all around, but there isn't *anybody!*" She prefers the noise and color of her "family"— the images on the television that call her by name.

As Montag despairs of reaching Millie, he recalls a man he met in a park a year ago, a retired English professor named

Faber who spoke to him in rhymeless poetry. At the end of their conversation the elderly professor had given Montag his address. Montag suspected the man owned books, so he had put the name and address in his notebook, but he had not turned the man in. Now he decides to visit Faber.

Faber knows Montag is a fireman, so he is afraid to let him in until he sees that Montag is carrying a book—the Bible. Faber eagerly turns its pages, wondering if God would recognize his own son as he is now portrayed in the media, as a subtle huckster for commercial products.

As Montag reveals the internal crisis that has brought him here, Faber tells him that books themselves are not the antidote to what ails him; books are merely the receptacles for "infinite detail and awareness," the places "where we stored a lot of things we were afraid we might forget." The magic is not in the books, but in how they stitched the universe together. Books, Faber says, are important because they preserve information, and they encourage people to take the time to think about things in a leisurely fashion. These gifts are only useful, though, if people have the right to act on what they learn from books.

Montag suggests that they begin to upset the social order by planting books in the home of every fireman and then turning in all the firemen. Faber argues that reviving civilization will not be so easy, since most folks are happy with the status quo. As they talk, planes are fighting overhead, and Faber says they should just let the war kill off the technological society. But when Montag threatens to destroy the Bible he brought with him, Faber relents and agrees to go along with the plan.

Montag fears that the smooth-talking Captain Beatty may persuade him to betray his new enthusiasm, and asks Faber for help in resisting. Faber brings out a tiny radio device that fits in Montag's ear; when Faber puts a second one in his own ear, they can speak to each other from a distance without detection. Faber says he'll help Montag maintain his perspective by talking to him as he deals with Beatty.

Back home, Montag is eating when Millie's friends, Mrs. Phelps and Mrs. Bowles, arrive to watch television with her. After a few minutes, Montag turns the TV off and asks the women when they think the war will start. The women claim they are not worried—the army says the war will last only a day or two, and anyway, if their husbands are killed, their lives will go on.

The women are clearly uneasy, both at the absence of noise and at Montag's insistence on conversation, but they answer his questions. One explains why she has no children; the second claims that children are really no bother, though on the few occasions when she sees hers, they seem to hate her. Millie suggests politics as a topic, and the women boast that in the last election they voted for the good-looking, well-groomed candidate with the noble name, rather than the fat one who mumbled.

Millie asks Guy to leave so they can return to their program, but he goes out only to fetch a book of poetry, which he insists on reading to the women. After he reads a poem, Mrs. Phelps begins crying and is unable to explain why. Mrs. Bowles denounces Montag for hurting her friend, and the two women leave.

Montag looks for his books and realizes Millie has burned some of them; he takes the rest and hides them outside, then leaves for work with Faber's whispered encouragement in his ear.

When Beatty sees Montag, he holds out his hand, and Montag hands him a book. The captain says he hopes Montag's "fever" is over and invites him to join the card game the firemen are playing. Montag is nervous, and Beatty begins baiting him, quoting lines about knowledge and truth from many different authors.

Faber tries to calm Montag. Just as Montag opens his mouth to respond to Faber—and thus reveal the secret radio in his ear—the fire alarm sounds.

Beatty drives the Salamander, as the fire truck is called, and Montag is stunned when their four-man team pulls up in front of his own house. Mildred comes out with a suitcase; she has turned him in, and is leaving him. She apparently watched him hide the books and retrieved them; now they litter the floor, their covers torn off.

Beatty insists that Montag set fire to his books himself, using the flamethrower to burn them individually rather than using kerosene. Faber, in his ear, urges Montag to run away; Montag cries out that he cannot, because of the Hound. Beatty, thinking Montag is talking to him, agrees that the Hound is nearby and warns him not to try anything. Montag sets the house afire, room by room, and Beatty tells him that when he is finished, he will be placed under arrest.

Again Montag hears Faber telling him to run away. Beatty sees him tilt his head, listening, and hits him so the radio flies from his ear. The captain picks up the radio, hears

Faber, and says they will come for him next. At the threat to his friend, Montag releases the safety catch on the flamethrower. Moving toward him, Beatty taunts him to pull the trigger, and Montag turns the flame on the captain, killing him. He knocks out the other two firemen but, before he can escape, he is attacked by the Mechanical Hound. He fights it off with the flamethrower, but not before it has injected him with a bit of its poison, which numbs his leg. He limps away, then returns to find a few books that Millie had missed near the garden fence. As he hurries away, he realizes that Beatty taunted him because he wanted to die.

Searching his pockets, he finds money he withdrew from the bank to finance the plan to plant books in firemen's homes and a thimble radio, on which he hears a police bulletin ordering his capture. As he flees, he realizes he is running to Faber's house, not because he believes the old professor can help him but simply because he wants to see him once more, to reinforce his faith that such people exist. As helicopters search for him, he makes his way to Faber's door, stopping on the way to plant one of his books in the home of a fellow fireman and to phone in an alarm to report the hidden book. On the way, he hears a news report that the war has begun.

When he arrives at Faber's, he reassures his friend that the radio device that could have betrayed him has been destroyed. Faber advises him to head for the river, and then follow the old railroad lines into the countryside, looking for hobo camps. The professor is leaving, too, heading for St. Louis to see a retired printer; they will use the money Montag gives him to begin printing books.

On Faber's small television, they follow the manhunt and learn that a new Mechanical Hound has been brought in to track Montag by his scent. Faber gives Montag some of his old clothes to put on later, tho throw the Hound off track, and Montag tells the professor how to remove the fugitive's scent from his home. Then he runs to the river, where he strips off his own clothes and dons Faber's. He walks into the river and allows it to carry him away. When he is three hundred yards downstream, he sees the Hound and the helicopters reach the river, then turn back toward the city, as if they have picked up the scent again.

Some time later, hearing no sounds of pursuit, he leaves the river and eventually comes upon the railroad track. As he follows it away from the city, he is suddenly certain that "once, long ago, Clarisse had walked here."

After a short time, he spots a fire in the woods. He approaches warily, then realizes this fire is warming rather than burning—a new perspective on the element that he has known only as a tool of destruction. Gathered around the fire are men in conversation; they call out to him to join them. They know who he is, and give him a chemical to drink that will keep the Hound from tracking him. On their portable, battery-powered television set, he sees the Hound attack and kill an unsuspecting stranger in the city as the announcer crows that it has caught and killed "Montag." The men explain that the government faked a quick, decisive resolution to the chase, and they point out to Montag that the face of the victim was never shown clearly.

The men then introduce themselves; most of them are former professors or authors. Each of them has memorized a book, to preserve the knowledge it contained, then burned the book so it cannot incriminate him. Montag says he has read Ecclesiastes, but protests that he cannot remember it all. The leader, Granger, tells him not to worry, because they have perfected a method of recovering the memory of any text that has been read once.

The group begins moving along the river, when suddenly, in the space of a few seconds, the war begins and ends. They see from afar the bombing of the city, which is completely destroyed; Montag realizes Millie has died, but is relieved to remember that Faber should be on a bus between cities, and thus safe. The group decides to turn back and find people who will need their help. Eventually, they hope, the books they carry inside them will help rebuild civilization.

CHAPTER 1

Symbol and Metaphor in *Fahrenheit 451*

READINGS ON

FAHRENHEIT 451

The Use of Fire as a Multifaceted Symbol

Donald Watt

Readers may expect a novel about burning books to use flame as a symbol of annihilation, but Donald Watt discusses how Bradbury uses fire as a metaphor for both destructive and creative potential. Watt, a professor of English at the State University of New York at Geneseo, has contributed essays to two volumes in the Writers of the 21st Century Series, *Ray Bradbury* (from which this essay is excerpted) and *Isaac Asimov.*

"It was a pleasure to burn," begins Bradbury's *Fahrenheit 451.* "It was a special pleasure to see things eaten, to see things blackened and *changed.*" In the decade following Nagasaki and Hiroshima, Bradbury's eye-catching opening for his dystopian novel assumes particular significance. America's nuclear climax to World War II signalled the start of a new age in which the awesome powers of technology, with its alarming dangers, would provoke fresh inquiries into the dimensions of man's potentiality and the scope of his brutality. . . . Montag's Nero complex is especially striking in the context of the looming threat of global ruin in the postwar era: "With the brass nozzle in his fists, with this great python spitting its venomous kerosene upon the world, the blood pounded in his head, and his hands were the hands of some amazing conductor playing all the symphonies of blazing and burning to bring down the tatters and charcoal ruins of history." Montag's intense pleasure in burning somehow involves a terrible, sado-masochistic temptation to torch the globe, to blacken and disintegrate the human heritage. . . . The opening paragraph of Bradbury's novel immediately evokes the consequences of unharnessed technology and contemporary man's contented refusal to acknowledge these consequences.

Excerpted from "Burning Bright: *Fahrenheit 451* as Symbolic Dystopia," by Donald Watt, in *Ray Bradbury,* edited by Martin Harry Greenberg and Joseph D. Olander (New York: Taplinger, 1980). Reprinted by permission of the author. (Endnotes in the original have been omitted from this reprint.)

In short, *Fahrenheit 451* (1953) raises the question posed by a number of contemporary anti-utopian novels. In one way or another, Huxley's *Ape and Essence* (1948), Orwell's *Nineteen Eighty-Four* (1948), Vonnegut's *Player Piano* (1952), Miller's *A Canticle for Leibowitz* (1959), Hartley's *Facial Justice* (1960), and Burgess's *A Clockwork Orange* (1962) all address themselves to the issue of technology's impact on the destiny of man. In this sense, Mark R. Hillegas is right in labeling *Fahrenheit 451* "almost the archetypal anti-utopia of the new era in which we live."[1] Whether, what, and how to burn in Bradbury's book are the issues—as implicit to a grasp of our age as electricity—which occupy the center of the contemporary mind.

THE ONLY MAJOR SYMBOLIC DYSTOPIA OF OUR TIME

What is distinctive about *Fahrenheit 451* as a work of literature, then, is not what Bradbury says but how he says it. With Arthur C. Clarke, Bradbury is among the most poetic of science fiction writers. Bradbury's evocative, lyrical style charges *Fahrenheit 451* with a sense of mystery and connotative depth that go beyond the normal boundaries of dystopian fiction. Less charming, perhaps, than *The Martian Chronicles*, *Fahrenheit 451* is also less brittle. More to the point, in *Fahrenheit 451* Bradbury has created a pattern of symbols that richly convey the intricacy of his central theme. Involved in Bradbury's burning is the overwhelming problem of modern science: as man's shining inventive intellect sheds more and more light on the truths of the universe, the increased knowledge he thereby acquires, if abused, can ever more easily fry his planet to a cinder. Burning as constructive energy, and burning as apocalyptic catastrophe, are the symbolic poles of Bradbury's novel. Ultimately, the book probes in symbolic terms the puzzling, divisive nature of man as a creative/destructive creature. *Fahrenheit 451* thus becomes a book which injects originality into a literary subgenre that can grow worn and hackneyed. It is the only major symbolic dystopia of our time.

The plot of *Fahrenheit 451* is simple enough. In Bradbury's future, Guy Montag is a fireman whose job it is to burn books and, accordingly, discourage the citizenry from

---

1. Mark R. Hillegas, *The Future as Nightmare: H.G. Wells and the Anti-Utopians,* New York: Oxford Univ. Press, 1967, p. 158

thinking about anything except four-wall television. He meets a young woman whose curiosity and love of natural life stir dissatisfaction with his role in society. He begins to read books and to rebel against the facade of diversions used to seal the masses away from the realities of personal insecurity, officially condoned violence, and periodic nuclear war. He turns against the authorities in a rash and unpremeditated act of murder, flees their lethal hunting party, and escapes to the country. At the end of the book he joins a group of self-exiled book-lovers who hope to preserve the great works of the world despite the opposition of the masses and a nuclear war against an unspecified enemy.

In such bare detail, the novel seems unexciting, even a trifle inane. But Bradbury gives his story impact and imaginative focus by means of symbolic fire. Appropriately, fire is Montag's world, his reality. Bradbury's narrative portrays events as Montag sees them, and it is natural to Montag's way of seeing to regard his experiences in terms of fire. This is a happy and fruitful arrangement by Bradbury, for he is thereby able to fuse character development, setting, and theme into a whole. Bradbury's symbolic fire gives unity, as well as stimulating depth, to *Fahrenheit 451*.

AN OPPOSITION OF FORCES

Bradbury dramatizes Montag's development by showing the interactions between his hero and other characters in the book; the way Bradbury plays with reflections of fire in these encounters constantly sheds light on key events. Clarisse, Mildred, the old woman, Beatty, Faber, and Granger are the major influences on Montag as he struggles to understand his world. The figure of Clarisse is, of course, catalytic; she is dominant in Montag's growth to awareness. The three sections into which Bradbury divides the novel are, however, most clearly organized around the leading male characters—Beatty in Part One, Faber in Part Two, and Montag himself (with Granger) in Part Three. Beatty and Faber—the one representing the annihilating function of fire, the other representing the quiet, nourishing flame of the independent creative imagination—are the poles between which Montag must find his identity, with Mildred and Clarisse reflecting the same polar opposition on another level. The men are the intellectual and didactic forces at work on Montag, while the women are the intuitive and experiential forces. Beatty articulates the system's point of view, but Mildred lives it. Faber articulates the opposition's point of view, but Clarisse lives it. Fire, color, light, darkness, and variations thereof suffuse Bradbury's account of the interplay among his characters, suggesting more subtly than straight dialogue or description the full meaning of *Fahrenheit 451.*

[A closer look at each of these three sections shows just how pervasive fire is in the narrative. Part One, provocatively entitled "The Hearth and the Salamander," presents crucial incidents which prod Montag out of the hypnotic daze of his fireman's existence. His meeting with Clarisse teaches him to be aware of life—or the lack of it—around him. His wife's brush with death, and the way she is saved, exposes for Montag the pitiable state of individual existence in their society. The stunning experience with the old woman at 11 North Elm demonstrates for Montag the possibility of defiance and the power of books. By the end of the section Montag's fireman foundations have been so rudely shaken that he wonders if "maybe it would be best if the firemen themselves were burnt."

Montag's initial encounter with Clarisse illustrates the care with which Bradbury arranges his narrative. . . . Against Montag's fierce, tight, fiery grin, Bradbury juxtaposes Clarisse's soft inner warmth. Hers is a gentle flame which promises more light to Montag than the inferno of the firemen: "Her face, turned to him now, was fragile milk crystal with a soft and constant light in it. It was not the hysterical light of electricity but—what? But the strangely comfortable and rare and gently flattering light of the candle." The thought reminds Montag of an incident in his childhood when, during a power failure, he and his mother lit one last candle and discovered "such illumination" in their quiet silence that they did not want the power to return too quickly. The figure of Clarisse glowing gently as a candle—slender, soft, serene—provides a marked contrast to the voracious acts of arson committed by the firemen. Montag thinks she is like a mirror "that refracted your own light to you." In his experience people were "more often—he searched for a simile, found one in his work—torches, blazing away until they whiffed out." In Montag's high-tension society, people burn themselves out from the inside, consumed by the ordained violence and mindless distractions certified by the authorities.

He searched for a simile, found one in his work. The appropriateness of Bradbury's symbolism consists of its logical derivation from Montag's perceptions, from his orientation and habits as a fireman. . . .

PART ONE: THE HEARTH AND THE SALAMANDER

Bradbury's symbolic language pervades and animates the first few scenes of *Fahrenheit 451*. The result is the creation of a mood or an aura about Montag's thoughts and experiences. The many passing strokes, hints, and suggestions of what is shaping Montag's mind—his many graphic responses in his own terms to experiences which are to him evocative, sometimes intangible and bewildering—are the key to Bradbury's distinctive style. Bradbury's figurative evocations bring the reader to the threshhold of Montag's inner self, "that other self, the subconscious idiot that ran babbling at times, quite independent of will, habit, and conscience." In Bradbury's opening pages the reader can detect, through the symbols which Montag draws out of his surroundings, a dawning awareness of his real psychic being pulsing beneath the rubble of his society. Bradbury has meticulously selected his symbols at the beginning of the book, for he will return to them and develop them to give *Fahrenheit 451* inner coherence, unity, and depth of meaning.

The old woman at 11 North Elm, for example, startles Montag by quoting Hugh Latimer's famous words to Nicholas Ridley as they were being burned alive for their unorthodox views in the sixteenth century: "we shall this day light such a candle, by God's grace, in England, as I trust shall never be put out." Like Latimer and Ridley, the old woman burns to death rather than sacrifice her views, her books. The Oxford heretics being burned at the stake were a flame whose light has not been extinguished since. Montag soon tells Mildred that the fire which killed the old woman smolders inside him and will "last me the rest of my life." As the firemen chop away at the old woman's house, Montag thinks this is a particularly difficult assignment: "Always before it had been like snuffing a candle." Usually the victims are taken away before their houses are put to the torch. But the old woman proudly defies the firemen and burns along with her books. She becomes a candle that perseveres and shines like a beacon in Montag's mind. One cannot help but associate her with Clarisse.

Beatty's visit to Montag's home, where he explains the rationale behind burning books for the good of society, is the culmination of Part One. Beatty's ever-present pipe is a symbol of his commitment to a life of burning. His face, with its phosphorescent cheeks, is ruddy from his proximity to flames. Like the iron dragon that transports his crew to their victims' houses, Beatty is always puffing forth great clouds of smoke. He constantly plays with "his eternal matchbox," which guarantees "one million lights in this igniter." Obsessed, Beatty strikes "the chemical match abstractedly, blow out, strike, blow out, strike, speak a few words, blow out. He looked at the flame. He blew, he looked at the smoke." Beatty is a salamander man, at home in fire and smoke. . . .

The meaning of the title, "The Hearth and the Salamander," for Part One now becomes clear. On one hand, the hearth evokes the warmth and friendliness of a good book by the fireside. By the hearth one silently explores, like Clarisse, without bias or haste, the meaning of experience. The hearth also suggests the heat of emotional and intellectual stimulation drawn by the reader from the creative fire of the writer. Montag's instinct is for the hearth, as he sits in his hall through a rainy November afternoon poring through the books he has hidden in the ventilator of the air conditioner. The salamander, on the other hand, is Beatty's preference; it is an emblem of the firemen. Unlike the hearth-dweller, the salamander does not sit next to the fire, but in it. Of course, salamanders can survive in fire; but Bradbury's point is that men are not salamanders. When immersed in fire, men are destroyed. If fire is viewed as Bradbury's emblem for technology, the message becomes obvious.

PART TWO: THE SIEVE AND THE SAND

The inner flame kindled in Montag by Clarisse and the old woman flares up in Part Two, as Montag comes under the illuminating influence of Faber. . . .

Bradbury develops Faber's position and impact on Montag by extending the applications of the novel's major symbol. As if in response to what Beatty says at the close of Part One, Faber tells Montag his view of their society's way of life: "They don't know that this is all one huge big blazing meteor that makes a pretty fire in space, but that someday it'll have to *hit*. They see only the blaze, the pretty fire, as you saw it." For Faber, the firemen's philosophy of eradicating knowledge for the contentment of the masses is merely a joyride of irresponsibility and evasion that is bound to end in a colos-

REBIRTH FROM FIRE: THE PHOENIX

Peter Sisario points out another important fire symbol:
that of the phoenix, which goes through an endless cycle
of death by fire and rebirth from its own ashes.

The major metaphor in the novel, which supports the idea of
the natural cycle, is the allusion to the Phoenix, the mythical
bird of ancient Egypt that periodically burned itself to death
and resurrected from its own ashes to a restored youth. Through
the persona of Granger, Bradbury expresses the hope that
mankind might use his intellect and his knowledge of his own
intellectual and physical destruction to keep from going
through endless cycles of disintegration and rebirth.

This image of the Phoenix is used in the novel in association with the minor character Captain Beatty, Montag's superior. As an officer, Beatty has knowledge of what civilization
was like before the contemporary society of the novel. . . . It is
crucial that Beatty wears the sign of the Phoenix on his hat
and rides in a "Phoenix car." He has great knowledge of the
past yet ironically and tragically does not know how to use his
knowledge, treating it only as historical curiosity. . . . He tells
Guy that fiction only depicts an imaginary world, and all great
ideas are controversial and debatable; books then are too in-
definite. Appropriately, Beatty is burned to death, and his
death by fire symbolically illustrates the rebirth that is associated with his Phoenix sign. When Guy kills Beatty, he is
forced to run off and joins Granger; this action is for Guy a
rebirth to a new intellectual life.

Peter Sisario, "A Study of the Allusions in Bradbury's *Fahrenheit 451*," *English*
Journal, February 1970.

sal smashup. Faber likes Montag's idea of planting books in
firemen's houses and turning in the alarm: "To see the fire-
houses burn across the land, destroyed as hotbeds of treason. The salamander devours his tail!". . .

Bradbury also extends his notion, introduced by Mildred's
overdose of sleeping pills, that Montag's society is consum-
ing and burying itself in fits of angst. Bradbury likens the
wild colors, savage music, and canned entertainment spew-
ing without end out of the multiwalled TV parlor to "an
eruption of Vesuvius." Mrs. Bowles and Mrs. Phelps arrive at
Montag's house to watch the White Clowns. With their
"Cheshire Cat smiles burning through the walls of the
house," they vanish "into the volcano's mouth." Bradbury's
figure conveys a sense of the ladies' immersion in a wash of

lava; they are already buried alive, like the citizens of Pompeii, under the ashes of the volcano that contains them. After Montag interrupts their programs, they sit in the parlor smoking cigarettes and "examining their blazing fingernails as if they had caught fire from his look." Representatives of all the masses living under the torch of organized violence and ever-impending war, the women are "burning with tension. Any moment they might hiss a long sputtering hiss and explode." Montag mercilessly exposes the ingrained fear, guilt, and anxiety with which they live and from which "the relatives" can only partially distract them. As Montag prepares to read Matthew Arnold's *Dover Beach*, the room is "blazing hot," he feverishly feels at once "all fire" and "all coldness," and the women wait "in the middle of an empty desert," sitting "in the great hot emptiness." Bradbury's symbolism is hard at work. Deprived of the White Clowns, the women feel abandoned as on a desert. On a desert there is no escape from the fiery sun—the scathing truths conveyed by Arnold's poem. In the reading, *Dover Beach* explodes through the veneers of superficiality protecting the women and confirms Montag's thought that the books in his house are dynamite which Mildred tries to disperse "stick by stick." Montag's angry outburst against Mrs. Bowles' protests releases some of his own pent-up heat. His rage is his first real spark of rebellion, and it soon fans into a hotter outburst against the unfortunate Beatty. . . .

Bradbury continues to play variations on burning in the final sequence of Part Two, where the two different, indeed opposite, kinds of flame flicker out at each other. Montag's return to the firehouse provokes Beatty to welcome him: "I hope you'll be staying with us, now that your fever is done and your sickness over." For Beatty, Montag's inner burning is the result of a fever. From Beatty's point of view, this burning means that a man has been unwell. But Montag wishes to nourish the burning; he doesn't want to return to normal. . . .

PART THREE: BURNING BRIGHT

The ramifications of Bradbury's two fires become clearer in Part Three, "Burning Bright," for the sequence of events portrays Montag's movement from one to the other, from the gorging arson of his own house to the comforting campfire of Granger. In this section Montag's growth develops into a belief in what Blake symbolizes in his poem, "The Tiger":

Tiger! Tiger! burning bright
In the forests of the night,
What immortal hand or eye
Could frame thy fearful symmetry?

Blake's tiger is the generative force of the human imagination, the creative/destructive force which for him is the heart of man's complex nature. Montag becomes Bradbury's tiger in the forests of the night. He becomes a hunted outcast from an overly tame society by making good his violent escape from the restraining cage of the city. In his rebellion and flight, Montag *is* burning bright. Paradoxically, the flame of his suppressed human spirit spreads through his whole being after his horrible murder of Beatty. In burning Beatty, Montag shares the ambivalence of Blake's tiger, with its symbolic combination of wrath and beauty, its "fearful symmetry."

Bradbury introduces another allusion, one connected with his major symbol, when the fire engine pulls up before Montag's house at the opening of the third section and Beatty chides him: "Old Montag wanted to fly near the sun and now that he's burnt his wings, he wonders why." Beatty's reference is to the mythological Icarus who soared into the sky with Daedalus, his father, on wax wings. But Icarus, carried away by the joy of flying, went too close to the sun, causing his wings to melt and making him fall. Clarisse, we recall, used to stay up nights waiting for the sunrise, and her face reminded Montag of a clock dial pointing toward a new sun. The sun, traditional symbol of truth and enlightenment, is antithetical to the dark night of ignorance that Beatty spreads across the land. The difference between Montag and Icarus—which, of course, Beatty will never live to see—is that Montag, though crippled by the Mechanical Hound, survives his own daring. Burning bright and living dangerously, Montag skirts the destruction Beatty plans for him and flees to the liberated periphery of society where pockets of truth endure undimmed.

At the beginning of Part Three, however, Beatty prevails. Montag once more enjoys the purging power of the fireman as he lays waste to his own house: "And as before, it was good to burn, he felt himself gush out in the fire, snatch, rend, rip in half with flame, and put away the senseless problem. . . . Fire was best for everything!" Montag destroys his house piecemeal, surprised that his twin beds go up "with more heat and passion and light than he would have supposed them to contain." Bradbury's lyrical style conveys Montag's fascination with the splendor and the transforming power of the flames. His books "leapt and danced like roasted birds, their wings ablaze with red and yellow feathers." He gives the TV parlor "a gift of one huge bright yellow flower of burning." Beatty affects Montag strongly with his enticing argument for burning:

> What is fire? It's a mystery. Scientists give us gobbledegook about friction and molecules. But they don't really know. Its real beauty is that it destroys responsibility and consequences. A problem gets too burdensome, then into the furnace with it. Now, Montag, you're a burden. And fire will lift you off my shoulders, clean, quick, sure; nothing to rot later. Anti-biotic, aesthetic, practical.

With a happy vengeance Montag levels the house where he has become a stranger to his own wife. He feels as though a fiery earthquake is razing his old life as Montag the fireman, burying his artificial societal self, while in his mind his other self is running, "leaving this dead soot-covered body to sway in front of another raving fool." Beatty cannot understand that at this point Montag is inwardly turning the flamethrower against its owners, that by burning his house he is deliberately destroying his niche in Beatty's system.

Only when Beatty threatens to trace Faber does Montag realize that the logical end to his action must be the torching of his chief. As Montag recognizes, the problem is, "we never burned *right. . .*". The shrieking, melting, sizzling body of Beatty is Bradbury's horrible emblem of the end result of a civilization based on irresponsibility. Beatty has always told Montag not to face a problem, but to burn it. Montag considers: "Well, now I've done both." One may conclude that Montag fights fire with fire.

The remainder of the novel consists of Montag's escape from the domain of the Mechanical Hound, his immersion in the countryside, and his discovery of Granger's group of bookish outcasts. . . .

A FRESH BEGINNING

At the very end, Bradbury does inject the promise of at least a seasonal renewal, and perhaps more, for man. As the men put out their campfire, "the day was brightening all about them as if a pink lamp had been given more wick." The candle figure is instructive, for it brings the reader all the way back to Clarisse and the kind, humane light she stands for. As they break camp the men, including Granger, fall in behind Montag, suggesting that he will become their leader. Montag, which means Monday in German, will conceivably light their way to a fresh beginning for man. As he wonders what he can say to make their trip up-river a little easier, Montag feels in his memory "the slow simmer" of words from the Bible. At first he remembers the initial verses from Chapter 3 of Ecclesiastes: "To everything there is a season. Yes. A time to break down, and a time to build up. Yes. A time to keep silence and a time to speak. Yes, all that." But The Preacher's words on the vanity of worldly things are not enough for Montag. He tries to remember something else. He digs into his memory for the passage from Revelations 22:2: *"And on either side of the river was there a tree of life, which bare twelve manner of fruits, and yielded her fruit every month; And the leaves of the tree were for the healing of the nations."* This is the thought Montag wants to reserve for noon, the high point of the day, when they reach the city. Bradbury draws on the Biblical notion of a heavenly Jerusalem, the holy city where men will dwell with God after the apocalypse. Its appeal for Montag is the final stroke of Bradbury's symbolism. In the Bible the heavenly city needs no sun or moon to shine on it, for God's glory is what keeps it lit. The nations of the Earth will walk together by this light, and there will be no night there. The light Montag bears in Granger's remnant of humanity is the Biblical hope for peace and immutability for mankind. This light is the permanent flame Montag has discovered in answer to the devouring nuclear burning invited by Beatty's society and as a counterpoint to the restless Heraclitean fire of the visible cosmos.

From its opening portrait of Montag as a singed salamander, to its concluding allusion to the Bible's promise of undying light for man, *Fahrenheit 451* uses a rich body of symbols emanating from fire to shed a variety of illuminations on future and contemporary man.[2]

2. Clearly there are many additional examples one could cite of Bradbury's uses of fire and its associated figures. An open book falls into Montag's hands at 11 North Elm and the words on the page "blazed in his mind for the next minute as if stamped there with fiery steel." In his initial talk with Montag, "Beatty knocked his pipe into the palm of his pink hand, studied the ashes as if they were a symbol to be diagnosed and searched for meaning." The Mechanical Hound comes sniffing at Montag's door, bringing "the smell of blue electricity." Mildred argues with Montag that the books will get them into trouble: "She was beginning to shriek now, sitting there like a wax doll melting in its own heat." Montag links his stumbling into Mildred's empty pillbox in the dark with "kicking a buried mine." When Montag first visits his house, Faber asks: "What knocked the torch out of your hands?" In rebuking Montag for falling under the influence of Clarisse, Beatty tells him such do-gooders "rise like the midnight sun to sweat you in your bed." As Montag prepares to cross the highway during his escape, he thinks it incredible "how he felt his temperature could cause the whole immediate world to vibrate."

Mirrors and Self-Examination in *Fahrenheit 451*

Rafeeq O. McGiveron

In *Fahrenheit 451* Bradbury uses mirrors both real and metaphorical to illustrate Guy Montag's growing impulse for self-examination, writes Rafeeq O. McGiveron. As he learns more about himself, Montag also finds mirrors in the characters of the other people in his life. McGiveron is an English instructor at Lansing Community College in Michigan.

In *Fahrenheit 451* Ray Bradbury creates an unthinking society so compulsively hedonistic that it must be atom-bombed flat before it ever can be rebuilt. Bradbury's clearest suggestion to the survivors of America's third atomic war "started . . . since 1990" is "to build a mirror factory first and put out nothing but mirrors . . . and take a long look in them." Coming directly after the idea that they also must "build the biggest goddamn steam shovel in history and dig the biggest grave of all time and shove war in and cover it up," the notion of the mirror factory might at first seem merely a throwaway line. Indeed, John Huntington suggests, with no little justification, that the whole passage is "Confuse[d]" by its "vagueness, ambiguity, and misdirection." Despite that, however, Bradbury shows throughout *Fahrenheit 451* the necessity of using a metaphorical mirror, for only through the self-examination it makes possible can people recognize their own shortcomings.

The novel's first use of the mirror, a failed one, emphasizes the need for self-examination. After a book burning, Guy Montag, the unsettled "fireman," knows "that when he return[s] to the firehouse, he might wink at himself, a minstrel man, burnt-corked, in the mirror." Montag's winking

From Rafeeq O. McGiveron, "'To Build a Mirror Factory': The Mirror and Self-Examination in Ray Bradbury's *Fahrenheit 451*," *Critique*, vol. 39, no. 3 (Spring 1998), pp. 282–87. Reprinted with permission from the Helen Dwight Reid Educational Foundation. Published by Heldref Publications, 1319 Eighteenth St. NW, Washington, DC 20036-1802. Copyright © 1998.

acceptance of himself here is not reflective but reflexive, for his glance is superficial rather than searching. Montag has the opportunity truly to examine himself, and if he did, he might see a glorified anti-intellectual stormtrooper. However, the situation, the surroundings, and even the mirror itself are too familiar, and he does not see himself as he really is. Instead of recognizing the destructiveness of his book-burning profession, his gaze is merely one of self-satisfaction.

Bradbury uses Clarisse, Guy's imaginative and perceptive seventeen-year-old neighbor, as a metaphorical mirror to begin reflecting truths that Montag otherwise would not see. The imagery of mirrors and reflection is very clear:

> He saw himself in her eyes, suspended in two shining drops of bright water, himself dark and tiny, in fine detail, the lines about his mouth, everything there, as if her eyes were two miraculous bits of violet amber that might capture and hold him intact.

Montag thinks of Clarisse again:

> How like a mirror . . . her face. Impossible; for how many people did you know who refracted your own light to you? . . . How rarely did other people's faces take of you and throw back to you your own expression, your own innermost trembling thought?

William F. Touponce suggests that Montag thereby receives "a tranquil affirmation of his being"; those passages bear that out.

But Clarisse's mirror imagery serves another function. Seeing himself in the mirror of Clarisse helps Montag realize that he merely "[wears] his happiness like a mask. . . ." He imagines that Clarisse has "run off across the lawn with the mask. . . ." It would, however, be more accurate to say that Montag himself throws away the poorly fitting mask after Clarisse shows, or reflects to him, the truth underneath. Clarisse's game of rubbing a dandelion under his chin to determine whether he is in love "sum[s] up everything," showing Montag an aspect of his emptiness he otherwise could not see. Her curiosity about why he and his wife have no children is another example of her mirror function. Perhaps most important, Clarisse asks about Montag's job: "How did it start? How did you get into it? How did you pick your work and how did you happen to think to take the job you have? . . . It just doesn't seem right for you, somehow." With each little observation, game, or question, Clarisse reflects a previously unseen truth for Montag to examine and, in the words of Robert Reilly, "show[s] him how empty his existence is."

A MIRROR TO SOCIETY

In addition to serving as a mirror reflecting Montag himself, Clarisse also serves as a mirror held up to the rest of society. Her perspective helps Montag see that his contemporaries, as Clarisse says, really neither talk nor think about anything; "No, not anything. They name a lot of cars or clothes or swimming pools mostly and say how swell! But they all say the same things and nobody says anything different from anyone else." That should be as familiar to Montag as the cloying stench of kerosene (of which Montag blithely observes, "You never wash it off completely"). Yet really to notice and examine those too-familiar facts he needs to see the situation reflected in the mirror of Clarisse.

Clarisse is a mirror not simply because she informs readers about the state of society. Each of the characters does that. If informing were the sole criterion for being a mirror, then even the most minor character would qualify—and so would most of the novel's narrative description. The metaphor would be so all-inclusive as to be meaningless. Clarisse is a mirror because she is so mirrorlike in her informing. She "talk[s] about how strange the world is," reminding Montag that "everyone . . . is either shouting or dancing around like wild or beating up one another," but she has no ideological agenda. For the most part Clarisse does not interpret or offer suggestions; she merely draws Montag's attention to facts he should already understand but does not. Like a mirror, Clarisse guilelessly reflects the truth into Montag's eyes.

Guy's wife, Millie, is another mirror, although Bradbury has not set her up with imagery like Clarisse's. Like the firehouse mirror, however, she is such a part of Guy's routine that he cannot seem to see what she reflects. In the beginning of the novel, Guy may find it "a pleasure to burn" books and may honestly claim that "[k]erosene . . . is nothing but perfume to me," but Millie finds even more pleasure in the burning. She compulsively watches her three-wall television and begs Guy for a fourth wall that would cost one-third of his yearly salary. When not entranced by the television, she wears "thimble radios tamped tight" in her ears, even in bed.

Sometimes while her husband sleeps she drives all night out in the country, "feel[ing] wonderful" hitting rabbits and dogs. She has begun to overdose on sleeping pills but still maintains in bland disbelief, "I wouldn't do a thing like that." Millie shows the superficiality and emptiness of the novel's society, yet Guy misses her mirror function. He finally recognizes her as "a silly empty woman" who is "really bothered," but he never seems to understand that she reflects an entire culture. As with the firehouse mirror, Montag has not looked carefully enough.

Beatty and Faber—chief book burner and former literature professor, respectively—both explain to Montag how the society of the past has turned into the inhumane world of *Fahrenheit 451.* Yet neither of those men is a mirror, for unlike Clarisse and Millie, they are overtly didactic. Each tries to sway Montag with a different interpretation of the past. Beatty wants Montag to "stand against the small tide of those who want to make everyone unhappy with conflicting theory and thought," whereas Faber has no plans but at least wants Montag to think. Although the two characters provide important historical and sociological information, they are teachers more than mirrors. As Donald Watt notes, Beatty and Faber articulate the ideas that Millie and Clarisse live. They reflect society to some extent, but more often they evaluate and advise—tasks of the viewer and thinker, not the mirror.

SELF-EXAMINATION

The book contains other important mirrors. After a week of daily talks with Clarisse, Montag is ready to look into one of them. This time he takes more initiative, for the mirror is one he must visualize himself. After ten years of simple acceptance, Montag finally sees himself by looking into the mirror of the other firemen:

> Montag looked at these men whose faces were sunburnt by a thousand real and ten thousand imaginary fires, whose work flushed their cheeks and fevered their eyes. These men who looked steadily into their platinum igniter flames as they lit their eternally burning black pipes. They and their charcoal hair and soot-colored brows and bluish-ash-smeared cheeks where they had shaven close. . . . Had he ever seen a fireman that *didn't* have black hair, black brows, a fiery face, and a blue-steel shaved but unshaved look? These men were all mirror images of himself!

Montag is [according to Watt] "appalled," for this mirror invites a disquieting self-examination.

After looking into the ready-made mirror of Clarisse and recognizing an unflattering image mirrored by the other mindless firemen, Montag begins holding up his own mirror to society. The first attempt, when he and Millie look through the books he has stolen, is a comparative failure. Guy tells Millie, "[Books] just *might* stop us from making the same damn insane mistakes [people have always made]!", but he cannot find a text that mirrors his own society clearly enough to provide either criticisms or solutions. Montag reads, "'It is computed that eleven thousand persons have at several times suffered death rather than submit to break their eggs at the smaller end.'" Swift's *Gulliver's Travels* may be, as Peter Sisario claims, "an excellent one for him to choose," but it is excellent for the well-read reader, not for Montag. The firehouse mirror and the mirror that is Millie are missed opportunities because Montag does not look hard enough, but this book-mirror may be too subtle for him even to recognize.

Despite that failure, Professor Faber reminds Montag that mirrors are all around him. Although he does not speak in terms of mirrors, the idea of the reflection of truths fills his discussion:

> "It's not books you need, it's some of the things that once were in books. The same things *could* be in the [televised] 'parlor families' today. The same infinite detail and awareness could be projected through the radios and televisors, but are not. No, no, it's not the books at all you're looking for! Take it where you can find it, in old phonograph records, old motion pictures, and in old friends; look for it in nature and look for it in yourself. Books were only one type of receptacle where we stored a lot of things we were afraid we might forget. There is nothing magical in them at all. The magic is only in what the books say, how they stitched the patches of the universe together into one garment for us."

Bradbury uses more than one type of imagery here, but the idea of the mirror could easily encompass them all. Throughout his talk Faber stresses examining the individual and society as reflected in a metaphorical mirror.

Faber says that books "can go under the microscope. You'd find life under the glass, streaming past in infinite profusion. The more pores, the more truthfully recorded details of life per square inch you can get on a sheet of paper, the more 'literary' you are." Reiterating that idea, he says that books "show the pores in the face of life." In other words, the microscope—or mirror—reflects important truths that otherwise would be missed. In that passage, Faber focuses on books; but his earlier discussion shows that a mirror can be found almost anywhere.

Finally, of course, Bradbury lets Montag stumble on a literary mirror that he, and even others, can recognize. When Guy reads Matthew Arnold's "Dover Beach" to Millie's friends, he holds up a mirror that reflects all too clearly:

> "'Ah, love, let us be true
> To one another! for the world, which seems
> To lie before us like a land of dreams,
> So various, so beautiful, so new,
> Hath really neither joy, nor love, nor light,
> Nor certitude, nor peace, nor help for pain;
> And we are here as on a darkling plain
> Swept with confused alarms of struggle and flight
> Where ignorant armies clash by night.'"

Beatty calls American civilization "our happy world," but families are hollow and loveless, suicide is commonplace, violence is endemic on the streets and in broadcast entertainment, and jet bombers circle ominously in the night. The poem's bleak conclusion rings so true that it makes the mindless Mrs. Phelps cry.

Just as Mrs. Phelps begins to get a glimmering of what it truly means to look in the mirror, Bradbury finally seems to allow Millie the same experience. As the bombs of one of the faceless enemies of an America that is "hated so much" abroad begin to fall on the city from which he has fled, Guy's fancy conjures up a most significant image:

> Montag . . . saw or felt, or imagined he saw or felt the [television] walls go dark in Millie's face, heard her screaming, because in the millionth part of time left, she saw her own face reflected there, in a mirror instead of a crystal ball, and it was such a wildly empty face, all by itself in the room, touching nothing, starved and eating of itself that at last she recognized it as her own.

Guy's peculiar little fantasy, of course, may not actually happen to Millie, but its existence demonstrates the crucial importance of the mirror. Unlike her husband, the imagined Millie of that passage recognizes its importance too late.

In the very last scene of the novel, Montag holds up the Bible as a mirror in which to see the world from a different perspective:

HOLDING A MIRROR UP TO THE AUTHOR
An author speculates on the depth of Bradbury's hatred for book burning.

Few things affected Ray Bradbury as traumatically as the Nazi book burnings. His wrath and indignation at this action, his conviction that civilization is today "burning" books; if not literally, then through neglect, recurs constantly in *Fahrenheit 451*. A psychologist might say that since writing offered Bradbury his one hope of immortality, the destruction or loss of public interest in the vehicles necessary to convey his thoughts virtually threatens his soul. The very idea is the theme of (his story) "The Exiles," where the spirits of great authors of the past vanish one by one as the final copies of their books are burned as the last person who remembers them dies.

Sam Moskowitz, *Seekers of Tomorrow: Masters of Modern Science Fiction.* Cleveland and New York: World, 1966.

> And when it came his turn, what could he say, what could he offer on a day like this, to make the trip a little easier? To everything there is a season. Yes. A time to break down, and a time to build up. Yes. A time to keep silence, and a time to speak. Yes, all that. But what else? Something, something. . . .

Ecclesiastes is a mirror providing some comfort, but Montag senses that Revelation is an even better one: *And on either side of the river was there a tree of life, which bare twelve manner of fruits, and yielded her fruit every month; And the leaves of the tree were for the healing of the nations.* Like Mrs. Phelps, he sees his own situation reflected in a piece of literature, but there the mirror brings hope rather than despair. Without the mirror of the Bible, however, Montag would be hard pressed to see any positive "truths" in his postnuclear world.

Granger, leader of the book-memorizing intellectuals whom Montag meets after his flight from the city, ties together all the other uses of mirror imagery. "Come on now, we're going to build a mirror factory first and turn out nothing but mirrors for the next year and take a long look in them." The suggestion reaffirms the necessity of using mirrors for self-examination. Just as Montag struggles to use figurative mirrors to discover the shortcomings in himself and in society, the survivors must use them in striving for a humane future. If they successfully use the mirrors, perhaps they can avoid making "the same damn mistakes."

Considered along with all the other mirrors in *Fahrenheit 451*, Granger's suggestion begins to make metaphorical · sense. Perhaps Bradbury's mirror imagery is not used as carefully as it could be; certainly it is possible to imagine its being more consistently employed or more fully articulated. Yet throughout the book, mirrors of a kind are missed and found, seen and used. With Montag's failures and successes, Bradbury shows that all of us, as individuals and as a society, must struggle to take a long, hard look in the mirror. Whether we look at ourselves from another's perspective or from the perspective of a good work of art, we need this self-examination to help avoid self-destruction.

WORKS CITED

Bradbury, Ray. *Fahrenheit 451.* 1953. New York: Ballantine, 1991.

Huntington, John. "Utopian and Anti-Utopian Logic: H.G. Wells and his Successors." *Science-Fiction Studies* 9 (1982): 122–46.

Reilly, Robert. "The Artistry of Ray Bradbury." *Extrapolations* 13 (1971): 64–74.

Sisario, Peter. "A Study of the Allusions in Bradbury's *Fahrenheit 451.*" *English Journal* Feb. 1970: 200+.

Touponce, William F. *Ray Bradbury and the Poetics of Reverie.* Studies in Speculative Fiction 2, 1981. Ann Arbor: UMI, 1984.

Watt, Donald A. "Burning Bright: *Fahrenheit 451* as Symbolic Dystopia." In *Ray Bradbury.* Writers of the 21st Century Series. Ed. Martin Harry Greenberg and Joseph D. Olander. New York: Taplinger, 1980. 195–213.

Montag's Spiritual Development

Wayne L. Johnson

Metamorphosis—the transformation of one thing into another—is a major theme of *Fahrenheit 451*, writes Wayne L. Johnson. As the hero, Montag, abandons the mechanical world, with its transforming, destructive fire and oppressive policies, and changes his life from book burner to book protector, he also undergoes a spiritual metamorphosis. Johnson is the author of the book *Ray Bradbury*, from which this essay is excerpted.

Fahrenheit 451 is one of only two novels Bradbury has written. The other is *Something Wicked This Way Comes.* (*Dandelion Wine* and *The Martian Chronicles* are often referred to as novels, but they are really collections of separate stories unified by theme and specially written bridge passages.) *Fahrenheit 451* is a short novel, an expansion of a story, "The Fireman," originally published in *Galaxy.* The book is about as far as Bradbury has come in the direction of using science fiction for social criticism. Actually, the premise of the book is rather farfetched—that firemen in some future state no longer fight fires but set them, having become arms of a political program aimed at stamping out all literature. This purging of the written word, particularly of the imaginative sort, is found in other stories, most strikingly in "Pillar of Fire" and "The Exiles." But in these other stories the tone is clearly that of a fantasy. *Fahrenheit 451* is realistic in tone, but keeps such a tight focus on the developing awareness of fireman Guy Montag that we can successfully overlook the improbability of his occupation. In fact, the very improbability of Montag's work allows Bradbury to maintain a certain detachment in the book, so that basic themes such as freedom of speech, the value of imagination, the authority of the state, individualism versus conformity, and so on, can be developed and explored without becoming either too realistic or too allegorical.

In the course of the book, Montag goes through what today might be called consciousness raising. He begins as a loyal fireman, burning what he is told to burn, progresses through a period of doubts and questioning, and ends up rebelling against the system and doing his part to keep man's literary heritage alive. But the bones of the plot do little to convey the feeling of the book. Bradbury's world here seems much closer to the present than the future—not so much in terms of its overall structure as in terms of its more intimate details. Some of the characterizations—Montag's wife, given over to drugs and mindless television; Clarisse, an archetypal hippie or flower child; and the old woman, who defies the firemen by pouring kerosene over her books and her own body before striking a match— might have been drawn from the turbulent political events of the sixties. It is almost necessary to remind oneself that *Fahrenheit 451* was published in 1953.

Many of Bradbury's pet themes are to be found in the novel. Metamorphosis is a major theme of the story, for in the course of it Montag changes from book-burner to living-book. Montag the fireman is intensely aware of the power of fire: "It was a special pleasure to see things eaten, to see things blackened and *changed.*" He himself is changed every time he goes out on a job: "He knew that when he returned to the firehouse, he might wink at himself, a minstrel man, burnt-corked, in the mirror."

Machines are of crucial importance. Overall, the book traces Montag's flight from the dangerous mechanical world of the city to the traditional haven of the country. Montag at first feels comfortable with machines, especially his flame-throwing equipment. The first time Montag meets Clarisse he views the scene in mechanical terms: "The autumn leaves blew over the moonlit pavement in such a way as to make the girl who was moving there seem fixed to a gliding walk, letting the motion of the wind and leaves carry her forward." But many mechanical things are repellent to Montag, particularly the equipment the medical technicians use on his wife after she has taken an overdose of sleeping pills: "They had two machines, really. One of them slid down your stomach like a black cobra down an echoing well looking for all the old water and the old time gathered there."

Montag's particular mechanical enemy is the fire station's

Mechanical Hound, more like a huge spider, actually, with its "bits of ruby glass and . . . sensitive capillary hairs in the Nylon-brushed nostrils . . . that quivered gently, gently, its eight legs spidered under it on rubber-padded paws." As Montag becomes more fascinated with books and nearer to betrayal of his duties as a fireman, the hound becomes more suspicious of him. The hound is then symbolic of the relentless, heartless pursuit of the State.

When Montag finally flees the city, he must first cross a mechanical moat, a highway 100 yards across on which the "beetle" cars seem to take pleasure in using pedestrians for target practice. Other machines Montag grows to hate are the radio and television that reduce their audience, Montag's wife, for one, into listless zombies.

SPIRITUAL DEVELOPMENT

But *Fahrenheit 451* is not primarily a work of social criticism. Its antimachine and antiwar elements are there primarily as background for Montag's spiritual development. It is interesting that this development seems to be in the direction of social outcast. Granted that Montag's society has its evils, but at the end of the book we are not so sure that Montag will be completely happy with his new-found friends, the book people. What we are sure of is that Montag has entrenched himself as nay-sayer to a society that has become hostile and destructive toward the past. Montag joins the book people whose task, as Granger puts it, is "remembering." But even as he does so, he promises himself that he will one day follow the refugees from the bombed-out city, seeking, though this is not stated, perhaps his wife, perhaps Clarisse. Most of the book people are like the old man in "To the Chicago Abyss," essentially harmless, using their talents for remembering things to aid their society in whatever way they can. But Montag may perhaps be too rigid an idealist, having rejected his former society with the same vehemence as he once embraced it. Like Spender in *The Martian Chronicles*, Montag has committed murder to maintain his freedom and the integrity of his vision. Unlike Spender, but like many of Bradbury's other outsiders and misfits, Montag has successfully achieved a truce or stalemate with a world hostile to his individuality. At the end of *Fahrenheit 451*, Montag's future can go either way; toward reintegration with a new, less hostile society, or toward a continuing, perpetual alienation.

The Power of the Wilderness in *Fahrenheit 451*

Rafeeq O. McGiveron

Nature in Bradbury's novel is not simply a metaphoric device that offers a pleasing contrast to Montag's artificial life in the city, notes Rafeeq O. McGiveron. The natural world in *Fahrenheit 451* is a wilderness that can be both attractive and awesome, even frightening. But facing that wilderness, McGiveron says, helps the hero understand his proper place in the world. McGiveron, who teaches at Lansing Community College in Michigan, has written on several aspects of *Fahrenheit 451*.

The importance of the wilderness in Ray Bradbury's 1953 *Fahrenheit 451* has been relatively ignored by critics, and when it has been discussed, this crucial subtheme has been distorted by oversimplification. Many have commented rather briefly upon Bradbury's depiction of the wilderness, but few go beyond seeing, as John Huntington does, that "nature is good and technology is bad." Certainly Bradbury shows nature to be preferable to the artificial sterility of the novel's compulsively hedonistic urban consumer society, yet he also wisely suggests that to be truly human we must know our place in the natural world not only by appreciating the beauties of the wilderness but by respecting its awesome power as well. The thoughtful and moral characters of the novel draw strength from the wilderness, and, when appropriate, they also respect and even fear it. It is this common approach to the world that makes them humane and admirable.

Clarisse McClellan, the inquisitive seventeen year old who helps the dissatisfied "fireman" Guy Montag turn away from his profession of burning books, illustrates how an ap-

Reprinted from Rafeeq O. McGiveron, "Do You Know the Legend of Hercules and Antaeus? The Wilderness in Ray Bradbury's *Fahrenheit 451*," *Extrapolation*, vol. 38, no. 2 (Summer 1997), pp. 102–109, by permission of The Kent State University Press. (References cited in the original have been omitted from this reprint.)

preciation of the wilderness helps lead to an understanding of one's place in the natural world. When she is first introduced, Bradbury characterizes her with very positive, lyrical nature imagery. Walking down a moonlit autumnal sidewalk, Clarisse, with her "slender and milk-white" face, seems as if she is "letting the motion of the wind and the leaves carry her forward." Less than two pages later her face is "bright as snow in the moonlight," "fragile milk crystal with a soft and constant light in it." Her eyes are like "two shining drops of bright water," "two miraculous bits of violet amber," and Montag can catch "the faintest breath of fresh apricots and strawberries in the air" even though it is "quite impossible, so late in the year." In the words of Donald Watt, "The meeting with Clarisse . . . introduces a contrast in Bradbury's narrative between the grimy, harsh, destructive milieu of the firemen and the clean, regenerative world of nature." Whereas Montag's colleagues all have "the colors of cinders and ash about them, and the continual smell of burning from their pipes," Clarisse is refreshing in her naturalness.

Just as she is associated so carefully with nature imagery, Clarisse happily and wisely appreciates the natural world. According to Clarisse, most of the scurrying inhabitants of the city fail to notice the natural beauties around them: "I sometimes think drivers don't know what grass is, or flowers, because they never see them slowly. . . . If you showed a driver a green blur, Oh yes! he'd say, that's grass!" Unlike the average citizen, however, Clarisse has seen the sunrise and has noticed the morning dew and the man in the moon. She knows that "rain feels good"and "even tastes good," "just like wine"—a positive thing to Bradbury—and she has found that old leaves "smell like cinnamon." She rubs a dandelion under her chin to discover whether she is in love and she often "hike[s] around in the forests and watch[es] the birds and collect[s] butterflies." She may kill a few colorful butterflies now and then, but Bradbury merely winks at this old-fashioned form of "appreciation."

Because she makes the effort to appreciate the many beauties of the natural world, Clarisse also has developed a far better understanding of her place in nature than the average person has. Her schoolmates, for example, obviously do not understand their natural capacity for humaneness, for they all are "either shouting or dancing around like wild or beating up one another." In a sense Clarisse truly is "let-

ting the motion of the wind and the leaves carry her forward," for she allows her human nature to guide her. It is
natural, for example, for humans to be curious and thoughtful, and one of the first things Montag notices about Clarisse
is that her "milk-white" face possesses "a kind of gentle
hunger that touche[s] over everything with tireless curiosity." Indeed, she questions much of the compulsive hedo-
nism of her society, not "want[ing] to know *how* a thing was
done, but *why*." Considered antisocial, Clarisse must see a
psychiatrist regularly, yet she tells Montag, "It's so strange.
I'm very social indeed. It all depends on what you mean by
social, doesn't it? Social to me means talking to you about
things like this." Clarisse's evaluation is correct, of course,
her understanding of human nature stemming at least in
part from her appreciation of the wilderness.

LEARNING TO THINK AGAIN

Clarisse's understanding of her place in nature benefits
Montag as well. Occasionally Montag finds "a bouquet of
late flowers on his porch, or a handful of chestnuts in a little sack, or some autumn leaves neatly pinned to a sheet of
white paper and thumbtacked to his door," all gifts from
Clarisse. In addition, more important than mere tokens of
friendship, Clarisse's example helps stimulate Montag to
wonder and to try new experiences. Even Clarisse notices it,
for she tells him that he is unlike the other "firemen" she
has met: "When I said something about the moon, you
looked at the moon, last night. The others would never do
that." Later, made curious by Clarisse, Montag tastes the
rain, and at Clarisse's urging he smells the leaves. Though
he claims feebly, "It's just I haven't had the time—,"
Clarisse's example shows him that there is more to life than
the moral and intellectual sterility of the unaesthetic work-
aday world. In other words, she helps him find his own
place in the natural world and thereby recognize the poten-
tials of his own human nature.

Fire Captain Beatty, the novel's chief book burner, mock-
ingly derides "that little idiot's routine. . . . Flowers, butterflies,
leaves, sunsets, oh, hell! . . . A few blades of grass and the
quarters of the moon. What trash. What good did she ever *do*
with all that?" One answer to Beatty's nervous question, of
course, is that unlike the majority of the population—Guy's
overdosing wife Millie, for example, who sees the wilderness

only as a place to "get [the car] up around ninety-five and . . . feel wonderful" hitting rabbits and dogs—Clarisse is truly happy. Whereas Beatty and the "firemen" burn down homes found to contain books while the owners are taken "screaming off to the insane asylum," Clarisse and her example help Montag learn to think again. Even Bradbury in his Afterword admits that Clarisse "verg[es] on silly star-struck chatter," but there can be little doubt that her simple appreciation of the wilderness nevertheless strengthens her humanity and Montag's also.

Donald Watt has noted that Faber, the old former literature professor who helps Montag learn to think again, is associated with "nature and natural smells." Although Faber "look[s] as if he ha[s] not been out of the house in years," Montag, significantly, first met Faber in a "green park a year ago." "They had sat in the soft green light. . . . His name was Faber, and when he finally lost his fear of Montag, he talked in a cadenced voice, looking at the sky and the trees and the green park." Along with symbolically associating Faber with nature, Bradbury demonstrates that the professor, like Clarisse—and unlike the mindless majority—appreciates the natural world and understands his place in it.

Even Faber's relationship to books is depicted with appreciative nature imagery. When Montag brings a Bible to Faber's house, Faber smells it lovingly: "Do you know that books smell like nutmeg or some spice from a foreign land? I loved to smell them when I was a boy." Watt, of course, already has drawn attention to this imagery of "natural smells." In addition, however, Faber describes books with a nice piece of visual nature imagery as well. According to Faber, "This book can go under the microscope. You'd find life under the glass, streaming past in infinite profusion." Though he is speaking figuratively, the vehicle of the metaphor is as valid as the tenor. A book is the product of technological manufacturing processes just as, say, the novel's four-wall televisors are, yet it is a coarser, homier kind of artifact, rough wood pulp rather than fired glass and vacuum-sealed electronics. Whereas Beatty praises fire for being "clean" and "antibiotic," Faber recognizes that humans are a part of nature and thus directly opposes such unnatural sterility, even at the microscopic and metaphorical level. Faber's microscope metaphor is surely the most subtle and unexpected piece of imagery tying together books and an understanding of the natural world, and to my taste it is also the most thematically effective.

In associating books with the natural world, Faber reflects Bradbury's narrative, wherein they are described with more poetic nature imagery. Throughout the novel books are "pigeon-winged," like "white pigeon[s] . . . [with] wings fluttering," "like slaughtered birds" whose pages are like "snowy feather[s]," and "like roasted birds, their wings ablaze with red and yellow feathers." Furthermore, Bradbury links books with nature again when Montag in a feverish daze takes the subway to Faber's house, illegal Bible in plain view in his hands, and the disillusioned "fireman" attempts in vain to consider the lilies of the field of Matthew 6:28.

CONNECTING WITH EARTH

In addition to employing this type of nature imagery, Bradbury eventually has Faber make the connection between humanity and the wilderness explicit. The old man asks Montag, "Do you know the legend of Hercules and Antaeus, the giant wrestler, whose strength was incredible so long as he stood firmly on the earth? But when he was held, rootless, in midair, by Hercules, he perished easily. If there isn't something in that legend for us today, in this city, in our time, then I am completely insane." Clearly Faber is not insane. He sees that "flowers are trying to live on flowers, instead of growing on good rain and black loam," because people refuse to recognize that "even fireworks, for all their prettiness, come from the chemistry of the earth." Faber knows that humanity cannot "grow, feeding on flowers and fireworks, without completing the cycle back to reality." Unlike Millie and Beatty, Faber appreciates the wilderness, and he knows his place in it as well.

After Montag finally kills the taunting, suicidal Beatty, he escapes into the wilderness which—rather improbably, considering that "there are billions of us and that's too many"— exists just on the edge of the city. Bradbury echoes the important dichotomy that Faber draws between "[t]he comfortable people" and the Antaeuses who understand their place in the natural world. Montag imagines the people of the city with "pale, night-frightened faces, like gray animals peering from electric caves," and when "in a sudden peacefulness" he floats away in the river, he feels "as if he ha[s] left a stage behind and many actors." Bradbury writes, "The river was mild and leisurely, going away from the people who ate shadows for breakfast and steam for lunch and vapors for supper. The river was very real; it held him comfortably and gave him the time at last, the leisure, to consider this month, this year, a lifetime of years." Whereas the city is shrouded by "the seven veils of unreality" and "the walls of [television] parlors," here "cows [chew] grass and pigs [sit] in warm ponds at noon and dogs [bark] after white sheep on a hill." In the words of William F. Touponce, Montag journeys to "the real natural world . . . outside the narcissism of the city," a place where people can have "a non-alienating relationship to nature."

Montag's flight from the city—which, coincidentally, is about to be atom-bombed by one of the many faceless enemies of an America that has "started and won two atomic wars since 1990"—reveals unmistakable imagery of the appreciation of the wilderness. When Montag startles a deer, Bradbury unleashes a heavy half-page of lingering description:

> He smelled the heavy musk like perfume mingled with the gummed exhalation of the animal's breath, all cardamom and moss and ragweed odor. . . .
>
> There must have been a billion leaves on the land; he waded in them, a dry river smelling of hot cloves and warm dust. And the other smells! There was a smell like a cut potato from all the land, raw and cold and white from having the moon on it most of the night. There was a smell like pickles from a bottle and a smell of parsley on the table at home. There was a faint yellow odor like mustard from a jar. There was a smell like carnations from the yard next door. He put down his hand and felt a weed rise up like a child brushing him. His fingers smelled of licorice.
>
> He stood breathing, and the more he breathed the land in, the more he was filled up with all the details of the land. He was not empty. There was more than enough here to fill him. There would always be more than enough.

John Huntington suggests that Bradbury's "purple rhetoric obscures true perception," and there is some truth in this. Some particulars may indeed be overdone examples of what Kingsley Amis calls "dime-a-dozen sensitivity"; certainly the idea of an endearing, childlike *weed* that smells of licorice is syrupy sweet. Yet despite such occasional problems of heavy-handed execution, Bradbury's emphasis on the necessity of appreciating the wilderness should not be dismissed so easily.

As with Clarisse and Faber, this appreciation helps lead Montag to an understanding of his place in the natural

world. Soon Montag "know[s] himself as a [sic] animal come
from the forest. . . . He [is] a thing of brush and liquid eye, of
fur and muzzle and hoof, he [is] a thing of horn and blood
that would smell like autumn if you bled it out on the
ground." Though Huntington must "take it that somehow
this reduction of the human to animal is somehow consoling and ennobling," it really requires no special stretch of
the imagination to see it as such. Clarisse already has
demonstrated that to truly appreciate the wilderness is to
have a better understanding of one's own humanity, and
Faber has asserted that one must not forget that humans are
a product of and a part of the natural world. Rather than "reduce" the human, Bradbury with this new image merely has
linked it more explicitly with nature.

RESPECT AND AWE FOR NATURE

While Montag is still in the city, Bradbury's nature imagery
consists mainly of that given by Clarisse and Faber. Once Montag escapes and begins to experience the wilderness for himself, however, Bradbury uses not only "purple rhetoric" but
imagery appropriate to respect and awe as well. In Bradbury's
scheme, the wilderness is not simply "good" and "nurturing"
(Huntington 137–38), a "refuge" (Mogen 109), "a regenerative
world" (Watt 199), "an arcadian utopia" (Touponce 83), or "a
new Eden" (McNelly 23); indeed, it can be all of those, but the
wilderness is also a force to be humbly respected. The only
critic to have commented upon this previously is George
Edgar Slusser, who merely notes with tantalizing brevity that
nature is dark, overwhelming, and immense (54). Examining
Bradbury's awed treatment of the wilderness in some detail is
worthwhile, however, for it reveals a significant attitude of humility and respect.

Bradbury shows that the second aspect of truly understanding one's place in nature is being humbled by the vast-
ness and power of the wilderness. When Montag first sees
the stars in the wilderness, undimmed by the light pollution
of the city, he sees not the pretty twinkling lights that readers might expect but "a great juggernaut of stars form in the
sky and threaten to crush him." Though the river in which
he floats seems comforting, the land seems a threatening
creature: "He looked in at the great black creature without
eyes or light, without shape, with only a size that went a
thousand miles, without wanting to stop, with its grass hills

and forests that were waiting for him." It is difficult to read this description as majestic or inviting, for the land's nightmarish darkness, its vast size, and its "waiting" seem brooding and ominous instead. When Montag finally steps ashore, the enormity of the wilderness is humbling: "The land rushed at him, a tidal wave. He was crushed by darkness and the look of the country and the million odors on a wind that iced the body. He fell back under the breaking wave of darkness and sound and smell, his ears roaring." Bradbury compares the "dark land rising" to "the largest wave in the history of remembering," which in his youth "slammed him down in salt mud and green darkness, water burning mouth and nose, retching his stomach, screaming! Too much water!" The ocean was fearsome to the child, and now to the adult there seems "too much land." Even the passage with the majestic, startled deer and the licorice-smelling weed that "rise[s] up like a child" describes the wilderness as a "huge night where trees ran at him, pulled away, ran, pulled away to the pulse of the heart behind his eyes"—definitely no "flowers, butterflies, leaves, sunsets" here.

Stumbling upon disused railroad tracks, Montag meets a former professor "significantly named Granger, a farmer, a shepherd guiding his flock [of book-memorizing intellectuals]" (McNelly 23). In a rather lengthy aside, Granger tells Montag about his grandfather, who

> hoped that someday our cities would open up more and let the green and the land and the wilderness in more, to remind people that we're allotted a little space on earth and that we survive in that wilderness that can take back what it has given, as easily as blowing its breath on us or sending the sea to tell us we are not so big. When we forget how close the wilderness is in the night . . . someday it will come in and get us, for we will have forgotten how terrible and real it can be.

While this passage seems to begin with mere appreciation, it soon shifts to humility and respect even more marked than that of Faber's story of Hercules. Though Granger's assertion that an "atom-bomb mushroom" seen from a V-2 rocket two hundred miles up is "a pinprick . . . nothing . . . with wilderness all around it" now seems dated in the age of the hydrogen bomb, in a wider sense his attitude of humility and respect toward a wilderness that might "someday . . . come in and get us" is still justified. Almost half a century after Bradbury wrote, the ravages of nature's "breath" may be more predictable, but they are no more controllable; moreover, if the camera in the nose of the V-2 were rotated up to look into the "juggernaut of stars," with its climate-wrecking meteors, its supernovas, and its quasars, Granger's awe of nature's power would seem even more justified.

A LAST, COMFORTING IMAGE

Despite such evidence of respect and even fear, Bradbury's last use of natural imagery is a comforting one. As Montag and the other book-memorizers walk back toward the atom-bombed city, blithely unconcerned with radiation poisoning, he remembers a passage from Revelations: *"And on the other side of the river was there a tree of life, which bore twelve manner of fruits, and yielded her fruit every month: and the leaves of the tree were for the healing of the nations."* This final piece of imagery reminds us, perhaps more directly than any other, that even though the natural world may be vast and sometimes threatening, it still can be a source of strength.

Bradbury's treatment of the wilderness in *Fahrenheit 451* is more complex and more true to life than it might first appear. Though his loving description of the wilderness and his persistent use of positive nature imagery clearly suggest that we should appreciate the natural beauties around us, Bradbury's careful reminders that the wilderness is vast and powerful should not be ignored. To be truly human we must know our place in the natural world, not only appreciating the wilderness but humbly respecting it, too. The humanity of Clarisse and Faber and Granger and Montag illustrate the benefits of understanding this—and the suicidal tendencies of the anesthetized Millie and the bitterly jesting Beatty reveal the grave dangers of forgetting it.

WORKS CITED

Amis, Kingsley. *New Maps of Hell: A Survey of Science Fiction.* 1960. New York: Arno, 1975.

Bradbury, Ray. *Fahrenheit 451.* 1953. New York: Ballantine, 1991.

Greenberg, Martin Harry, and Joseph D. Olander, eds. *Ray Bradbury.* Writers of the 21st Century Series. New York: Taplinger, 1980.

Huntington, John. "Utopian and Anti-Utopian Logic: H.G. Wells and his Successors." *Science-Fiction Studies* 9 (July 1982): 122–48.

McNelly, Willis E. "Ray Bradbury—Past, Present, and Future." In Greenberg and Olander, eds., 17–24.

Mogen, David. *Ray Bradbury.* Twayne's United States Authors Series 504. Boston: Twayne, 1988.

Slusser, George Edgar. *The Bradbury Chronicles.* Mitford Series, Popular Writers of Today 4. San Bernardino: Borgo, 1977.

Touponce, William F. *Ray Bradbury and the Poetics of Reverie.* Studies in Speculative Fiction 2. 1981. Ann Arbor: UMI, 1984.

Watt, Donald. "Burning Bright: *Fahrenheit 451* as Symbolic Dystopia." In Greenberg and Olander, eds., 195–213.

The Book's Censorship Metaphor Does Not Work—but the Movie Is Worse

Pauline Kael

Bradbury's idea of censorship lacks depth, charges well-known film critic Pauline Kael. But even worse is the on-screen depiction of the renegades' solution to book burning—to have people "become" books. An issue intended to be serious becomes comic at the thought that people might devote their lives to some of the volumes shown burning on-screen. Kael also objects to François Truffaut's flat direction and the actors' deadpan delivery; an issue that provokes such passion in real life, she asserts, should also seem passionately important on-screen.

There are some rather dumb—but in a way brilliant—gimmicks that have a strong, and it would almost seem a perennial, public appeal. Books or plays or movies based on them don't even have to be especially well done to be popular: readers and audiences respond to the gimmick. Sometimes this kind of trick idea is so primitive that it's particularly attractive to educated people—perhaps because they're puzzled by why they're drawn to it and so take it to be a much more complex idea than it is. *Frankenstein* is one of these fantastic, lucrative "ideas"; *The Pawnbroker* is almost one. A classic example of the use of one of them is Albert Lewin's 1945 movie adaptation of *The Picture of Dorian Gray*. Even the basic notion of Dorian Gray's remaining young and fresh and handsome while his portrait aged with the ravages of his evil soul wasn't sustained in the production—Hurd Hatfield's Dorian was never really young: he looked waxy and glacéed from the outset; and the other characters didn't age any more than he did. But audiences responded to the appeal of the idea, anyway, and are still responding to it on television re-runs and still arguing about how it should have been cast and carried out.

Dumb but Brilliant

François Truffaut's *Fahrenheit 451* isn't a very good movie but the idea—which is rather dumb but in a way brilliant—has an almost irresistible appeal: people want to see it and then want to talk about how it should have been worked out. *Fahrenheit 451* is more interesting in the talking-over afterward than in the seeing. The movie is about a society in which books are forbidden, not censored or rewritten as in Orwell's vision of 1984, but simply forbidden, burned. Book lovers run off to the woods where each memorizes a book and they become a living library. It is in the difference between the movie's simple gimmick-idea and Orwell's approach to censorship as an integral part of totalitarianism that we can see some of the weakness of the idea. Stripped of the resonances of politics and predictions and all those other repressions and forms of regimentation which are associated with book burning, the idea is shallow: it operates in a void. The strength of the idea is that in removing book burning from any political context, in using it as an isolated fearful fancy, it turns into something both more primitive and superficially more sophisticated than a part of a familiar, and by now somewhat tiresome, political cautionary message.

Of course, a gimmicky approach to the emptiness of life without books cannot convey what books mean or what they're *for:* homage to literature and wisdom cannot be paid through a trick shortcut to profundity; the skimpy science-fiction script cannot create characters or observation that would make us understand imaginatively what book deprivation might be like. Among the books burned are Poe's *Tales of Mystery and Imagination* and *The Martian Chronicles* by Ray Bradbury, who also wrote the book of *Fahrenheit 451.* This decorative little conceit has the effect of making us more aware than ever of the coyness and emptiness and inadequacy of the central conceit. The idea that one of the book people at the end might be devoting his life to preserving a text by Ray Bradbury (or *No Orchids for Miss Blandish,* which we also see in flames) is enough to turn the movie into comedy. The next step is to imagine all the jerks we've known and what they might give their lives to preserving— *Anthony Adverse? Magnificent Obsession? The Robe? The Adventurers? Valley of the Dolls?* We have only to think about it to realize how absurd the idea is. Why should a society burn all books on the basis that books make people think and so disturb them and make them unhappy? Most books don't make people think, and print is not in itself a danger to totalitarianism. That is a crotchety little librarian's view of books. Print is as neutral as the television screen. And so we're back from the primitive appeal of the gimmick, to the Orwell vision of censorship and terror. And yet such is the power of the gimmick that I swear I heard people in the theatre murmur at the astuteness of that nonsensical explanation for book burning. You'd think they'd never read a book, they're so willing to treat books as magical objects. And that is, of course, how the movie treats them: the gimmick turns books—any books—into totems, and this is part of the gimmick's appeal to educated audiences, probably a stronger appeal than a more rational treatment of the dangers of censorship could make.

LIBERAL HYSTERIA

Book burning taps a kind of liberal hysteria and the audience supplies the fearful associations: Hitler, McCarthy (who was the inspiration for the book, which was published in 1953). A woman who taught at Berkeley dropped in on me once and saw a book burning in the fireplace. She pointed at it in terror. I explained that it was a crummy ghost-written life of a movie star and that it was an act of sanitation to burn it rather than sending it out into the world which was already clogged with too many copies of it. But she said, "You shouldn't burn books" and began to cry. It's because of this kind of reaction, and because we don't think of book burning in a vacuum but of the historical horrors of taking away peoples' treasured possessions, of burning part of them, and of burning them, too, that the buggy little idea behind this movie is not easy to dismiss. *Frankenstein* preyed upon both our most primitive fears that man should not play God and our rather more sophisticated anxieties about scientists messing around with the order of things. *The Picture of Dorian Gray* brought back our childish fears that the bad secret things we did would show on our faces, as well as the more sophisticated fear, and perhaps envy, of all those beautiful people who could get away with murder, who could be ruthless and rotten and it would never show on their ingenuous faces. The banal suburban look of the future in *Fahrenheit 451* affects us at childish levels, too. The characters don't seem quite grown-up, and the notion of how to save books is peculiarly naïve—as in a fairy tale. The book people are a kid's idea of how to keep literature alive. They have no concept of carrying on a living literary tradition, of writing books, or of using books for knowledge or even against the state, but of turning themselves into books—as in a kids' game. Their notion of literature is a neighborhood library, and the book people at the end are coy and harmless eccentrics—bookworms.

For American art-house audiences who are both more liberal and more bookish than the larger public, book burning is a just-about-perfect gimmick. Yet even at the science-fiction horror-story level, this movie fails—partly, I think, because Truffaut is too much of an artist to exploit the vulgar possibilities in the material. He doesn't give us pace and suspense and pious sentiments followed by noisy climaxes; he is too tasteful to do what a hack director might have done. One can visualize the scene when the hero, Oskar Werner, reads his first book, *David Copperfield*, as it might have been done at Warner's or MGM in the thirties, how his face would light up and change with the exaltation of the experience— the triumph of man's liberation from darkness. Well, ludicrous as it would have been, it might have been better than what Truffaut does with it—which is nothing. Truffaut is so cautious not to be obvious, the scene isn't dramatized at all, and so we're left to figure out for ourselves that Werner must have enjoyed the reading experience because he goes on with it. Soon we're left to figure out for ourselves why he has gotten so addicted to books that he's willing to kill for them. It would, no doubt, be obvious to have an adulterous romance between Werner and the girl who goads him to read, but Truffaut doesn't supply *any* relationship to help define their characters. And if he feels that too much characterization is wrong for the genre, couldn't he at least give them actions that would define their roles in the story? Yes, it would be too much of a movie cliché to have Julie Christie play the two roles of the wife and the book girl in sharply contrasting styles; but Truffaut makes nothing out of her being so much the same in both roles. It hardly helps us to see what books mean in human life if her range of expressiveness is as narrow for the book girl as for the bookless, pill-head wife. The book girl's language is just as drab and she doesn't show any of the curiosity or imagination that might indicate that books had done something for her. Couldn't she have some quality that would help us understand why Werner reacts to her suggestion that he read a book? And shouldn't he have something that sets him apart, that makes him a candidate for heresy?

THE BOOK PEOPLE SHOULD SHOW THEIR LOVE OF WORDS

If the reply is that in this movie the books represent the life that is not in the people, then surely it is even more necessary to see that the book people have life. Shouldn't they speak differently from the others, shouldn't they take more

THE AUTHOR WAS PLEASED WITH THE DIRECTOR

Although many have found fault with director François Truffaut's movie version of Fahrenheit 451, *the author pronounced himself well pleased.*

François Truffaut seemed to have everything going for him.

Fortunately for all who have seen the movie on theater and television screens, the French director kept a diary from January 10 to June 21, 1966, the period of shooting. The diary, published in Numbers Five, Six, and Seven of *Cahiers du Cinema in English*, offers uncommonly interesting reading for those who have wondered what it's like to direct a movie. . . .

Reading the diary one will understand why film is a director's medium. And, since Truffaut had control over every phase of the film—from its photography to its special effects—*Fahrenheit 451* can truly be called *his* film.

The diary reveals every detail involved in the production. To the person who has seen the film and wondered why Julie Christie (both as the wife and Clarisse) and Oskar Werner did not relate to each other, the journal provides the answer: Truffaut had difficulty directing Werner. The diary reveals the director's and star's conflicts on the set. No matter what he might think of Werner's performance, though, the perceptive viewer could probably find faults with the film.

What are they? Some of the cast members perform with such uncertainty that one wonders if they understood their roles. At least one process shot—on the monorail where Montag first pleasure in language? Couldn't they give themselves away by the words they use—the love of the richness of words? It's all very well for the director not to want to be obvious, but then he'd better be subtle. He can't just abdicate as if he thought it would be too vulgar to push things one way or another. Criticism, in this case, turns into rewriting the movie: we can generally see what was intended but we have to supply so much of the meaning and connections for ourselves that it's no wonder that when it's over we start talking about how we would have done it.

There are a few nice "touches": the loss of memory by bookless people so that they have no past and no history; their drugged narcissistic languor; and there is the rather witty bit about the chief book burner (Cyril Cusack) seeing the proof of the worthlessness of books in the fact that writers disagree. But these touches are made to pass for more

meets Clarisse—is so ineptly handled that all but the most inexperienced viewer will detect that a scene was projected on a screen in back of the actors. The manner in which the Book People introduce themselves (one brother is *Pride;* his twin is *Prejudice*) is so coy that it dulls the intended impact. . . .

Perhaps the viewer will detect how the movie differs from the novel. It might well be he will think the only similarity is the idea of a society in which people are forbidden to read. (That is why the screen credits at the beginning of the film are spoken, not printed.) How faithful was Truffaut's film to Bradbury's novel? The director has hinted: "Now, on the screen you will see only what was in our two heads, Bradbury's brand of lunacy and then mine, and whether they have blended well."

And how happy was the author with the film adaptation of his work? Ray Bradbury has stated the answer:

"I have heard those cries in the past of outraged authors whose books have just been ruined by a studio.

"Such is not the case, luckily, with me.

"I think that Truffaut has captured the soul and essence of the book. He has been careful and subtle in his shadings and motions. He has escaped making a technological James Bond film, and made, instead, the love story of, not a man and a woman, but a man and a library, a man and a book."

Michael E. Keisman and Rodney E. Sheratsky, *The Creative Arts: Four Representative Types.* New York: Globe Book Co., 1968.

than they should because there aren't enough of them. The movie is so listless we have what we should never have in a gimmicky thriller: time to notice inconsistencies. People know how to read; why are they taught? Why are the book people hiding libraries in town instead of smuggling them to the woods? (Do they have a secret lending library?) Why are we shown the hero revealing his guilt to his co-workers (in scenes like his inability to go up the fire pole) if it doesn't lead to any consequences? Why are we shown an antagonism between Werner and another fireman (Anton Diffring) which never develops into anything functional in the structure? Why is it so easy to escape to the woods? Couldn't Truffaut or anyone think up a better contrivance to bring the book girl back than the need to retrieve an incriminating list of names (of people who memorize books!)? The actions in this movie don't flow from the theme; O.K., we can accept that if, at least, they're ingenious. But they're not. Still, all the holes in the plot would just make it seem lacy and airy if the movie had rhythm, if it moved purposefully, if the moods surprised us or intrigued us. Why doesn't it?

True, this film is the first Truffaut has made in a studio, the first in color (which slows down and complicates shooting), and it was made in England, with English technicians, and in English (thought Truffaut does not speak the language), which helps to explain why the timing and inflections are off in the dialogue and why the script sounds as if it were written by the bookless people. In other words, he has been totally uprooted and separated from his earlier co-workers. Business conditions made him a refugee, struggling against the same pressures of speed and efficiency and fixed shooting schedules that made the great refugee directors of Europe into modestly talented hacks in Hollywood in the thirties and forties, and so we cannot expect the spontaneity of *Shoot the Piano Player* and *Jules and Jim.* But not even a little bit of it? Truffaut *wanted* to make *Fahrenheit 451:* why then, even allowing for the hurdles of language and technology, isn't it more imaginatively thought out, felt, why are the ideas dull, the characters bland, the situations (like the hero breaking into the chief's office) flat and clumsy? Why is the whole production so unformed?

I would offer the guess that it's because Truffaut, in his adulation of Alfred Hitchcock, has betrayed his own talent— his gift for expressing the richness of life which could make him the natural heir of the greatest French director of them all, Jean Renoir. Instead, he is a bastard pretender to the commercial throne of Hitchcock—and his warmth and sensibility will destroy his chances of sitting on it. (Roman Polanski and dozens of others will get there before him.) Truffaut can't use Hitchcock's techniques because they were devised for something tightly controlled and limited and because they are based on coercing the audiences' responses (and, of course, making them enjoy it). Hitchcock is a master of a very small domain: even his amusing perversities are only two- or three-dimensional. Truffaut has it in him not to create small artificial worlds around gimmicky plots, but to open up the big world, and to be loose and generous and free and easy with it.

CHAPTER 2

Dystopia and Utopia

READINGS ON
FAHRENHEIT 451

A Condemnation of Consumerism

David Seed

The society portrayed in *Fahrenheit 451* counts consumption as its highest goal, notes David Seed. Everyday life has become divorced from political reality—even the reality of constant war—while the destruction of most printed material and state control of the rest discourage independent thought and action. The somewhat hopeful ending makes the idea of a simpler life seem appealing, a nostalgic notion of America's agrarian past.

Surveying the American scene in 1958, Aldous Huxley recorded his dismay over the speed with which *Brave New World* was becoming realized in contemporary developments: "The nightmare of total organization, which I had situated in the seventh century After Ford, has emerged from the safe, remote future and is now awaiting us, just around the next corner."[1] Having struck a keynote of urgency Huxley then lines up a series of oppositions between limited disorder, individuality and freedom on the one hand, and order, automatism and subjection on the other in order to express his liberal anxieties that political and social organization might hypertrophy. Huxley sums up an abiding fear which runs through American dystopian fiction of the 1950s that individuals will lose their identity and become the two-dimensional stereotypes indicated in two catch-phrases of the period: the "organization man" and the "man in the grey flannel suit." William H. Whyte's 1956 study diagnoses the demise of the Protestant ethic in American life and its replacement by a corporate one which privileges "belongingness." The result might be, he warns, not a world controlled by self-evident enemies famil-

1. Aldous Huxley, *Brave New World Revisited* (1958; rept. New York: Harper and Row, 1965), 4.

Excerpted from David Seed, "The Flight from the Good Life: *Fahrenheit 451* in the Context of Postwar American Dystopias," *Journal of American Studies*, vol. 28, no. 2 (1994), pp. 225–240. Copyright © 1994 Cambridge University Press. Reprinted by permission of Cambridge University Press.

iar from *Nineteen Eighty-Four*, but an antiseptic regime presided over by a "mild-looking group of therapists who, like the Grand Inquisitor, would be doing what they did to help you."[2] Whyte endorsed the social insights of Sloan Wilson's 1955 novel *The Man in the Grey Flannel Suit* which dramatizes the conflicts within the protagonist between individual advancement and self-location within a business hierarchy. Despite being an apparently successful executive Thomas Rath registers a tension between satisfaction and its opposite which recurs throughout fifties dystopias.

One crucial sign of this issue is the fact that the protagonists of dystopias are usually defined in relation to organizational structures. Walter H. Miller's 1952 short story "Conditionally Human" is typical of the genre in centering on an official. The action takes place in an America of the near future which has become "one sprawling suburb" ruled over by "Uncle Federal." Because the inexorable rise in the population is clearly threatening the promise of the "good life" the regime introduces draconian limits to the birth rate and the government-sponsored organization Anthropos Inc. designs baby substitutes called "neutroids", chimp-like creatures produced by the radioactive mutation of reproductive cells. The central character Norris has the job of an updated dog-catcher, rounding up stray "neutroids" to his wife's disgust. Already we can see the key generic motifs emerging: the problem of homogeneity, the disparity between restriction and avuncular government, the risk of technology exceeding its moral bounds, and—within the Norris couple—the debate between acceptance and dissatisfaction. When questioned by his wife, Norris characteristically pleads helplessness by appealing to the necessities of the system: "And what can I do about it? I can't help my Placement Aptitude score. They say Bio-Authority is where I belong, and it's to Bio I have to go. Oh, sure, I don't *have* to work where they send me. You can always join the General Work Pool, but that's all the law allows, and GWP'ers don't have families. So I go where Placement Aptitude says I'm needed."[3] Psychometrics has become institutionalized into a narrow series of legally enforced prescrip-

2. William H. Whyte, *The Organization Man* (1956; rept. Harmondsworth: Penguin, 1960), 33. The term "belongingness" was first used in the 1930s by the behavioural psychologist E.L. Thorndike. Its earliest postwar citations by the *O.E.D.* are by David Riesman (a contribution to A.W. Loos's *Religious Faith and World Culture*, 1951) and Whyte's *Invisible Man*. 3. Walter M. Miller, Jr., *Conditionally Human* (1962; rept. London: Science Fiction Book Club, 1964), 8.

tions which induce an acquiescence in Norris reflected in the key verb "belongs."

The adjustment of the individual's notion of appropriateness to officially measured norms evident in the story just quoted also figured prominently in the sociologist Mordecai Roshwald's examination of American society in the late fifties. Viewing developments with the special clarity of a newcomer (Roshwald was born in Poland and lived in Palestine before he took up permanent residence in the USA), he applied David Riesman's notion of other-directedness and located a resultant tendency to "imitation and uniformity." His 1958 article "Quo Vadis, America?" concludes with an indignant polemic against the complacency of imagining that the only danger confronting society is the external physical threat of atomic war. Not so. "The loss of individual norms in moral issues, the admiration of unjust power, the lack of tradition" and a host of other dangers present themselves just as urgently, and Roshwald here opens up a potential purpose for the writer of dystopias: "to warn against these and to fight them may be a second front in the fight for human survival. . . ."[4] Roshwald was in fact already contributing to that fight by working on his own dystopian novel *Level 7* (1959) which transposed the streamlined production systems of *Brave New World* on to the self-contained mechanized environment of a nuclear defence bunker. The inordinate reliance on technology and bland interchangeability of American manners which "seemed to point to a uniformly happy, efficient and self-sufficient society, verging on automata or robots," finds its expression in the novel as an ironic implication that the operative-protagonist is an extension of his machines instead of vice versa.[5] As happens with Montag in *Fahrenheit 451*, X-127, known only by his functional label, comes gradually to realize the consequences of his participation in a system, here of nuclear destruction, but with the added irony that his realization comes too late to make any difference even to his own fate. Roshwald's original title for this work was *The Diary of Push-Button Officer X-127* which appropriately stressed the issues of robotization, partly problematizing the individual's relation to technology and partly using that tech-

4. Mordecai Roshwald, "Quo Vadis, America?" *Modern Age*, 2.ii (1958), 195, 198. 5. Roshwald, letter of 1988, quoted in H. Bruce Franklin, "Afterword," *Level 7*, by Mordecai Roshwald (Chicago: Chicago Review Press, 1989), 190. This edition corrects errors which appeared in the original 1959 edition of the novel.

nology as a metaphorical expression of the individual's conformity to prescribed roles.[6] Quite independently Erich
Fromm identified the emergence of exactly the same social
type, declaring: "Today we come across a person who acts
and feels like an automaton; who never experiences anything
which is really his; who experiences himself entirely as the
person he thinks he is supposed to be."[7]

FAHRENHEIT 451 GOES ONE STEP FARTHER

Ray Bradbury's *Fahrenheit 451* (1953) goes one step farther.
Not only is the protagonist Montag initially a robot too, he is
also a member of the state apparatus which enforces such
prescriptions by destroying the books which might counteract
the solicitations of the media. The regime of the novel masks
its totalitarianism with a facade of material prosperity. Montag's superior Beatty explains its coming-into-being as a benign process of inevitable development, everything being justified on the utilitarian grounds of the majority's happiness:
"technology, mass exploitation, and minority pressure carried
the trick, thank God." A levelling-down is presented as a triumph of technological know-how and of system; above all it
was a spontaneous transformation of society not a dictatorial
imposition ("it didn't come from the Government down").
Bradbury's description of the media draws on *Brave New
World* as confirmed by postwar developments in television.
Observing the latter boom in America, Huxley commented:
"In *Brave New World* non-stop distractions of the most fascinating nature . . . are deliberately used as instruments of policy, for the purpose of preventing people from paying too
much attention to the realities of the social and political situation." He continues in terms directly relevant to the world of
Bradbury's novel: "A society, most of whose members spend a
great deal of their time . . . in the irrelevant other worlds of
sport and soap opera . . . will find it hard to resist the encroachments of those who would manipulate and control
it.". . .[8]

The result of this process in *Fahrenheit 451* is a consumer
culture completely divorced from political awareness. An au-
ral refrain running through the novel is the din of passing

6. Letter from Mordecai Roshwald, 29 April, 1993. I have discussed these themes in
greater detail in "Push-Button Holocaust: Mordecai Roshwald's *Level 7*," *Foundation*,
57 (Spring 1993), 68–86. 7. Erich Fromm, *The Sane Society* (London: Routledge and
Kegan Paul, 1956), 16. 8. Huxley, 37.

bombers which has simply become background noise. This suggests a total separation of political action from everyday social life and correspondingly when Montag's wife Millie and her friends agree to "talk politics" the discussion revolves entirely around the names and appearances of the figures concerned. In other words the latter have become images within a culture dominated by television. . . .

Montag's living room has become a 3-D televisual environment for his wife who dreams of adding a fourth wall-screen so that the house will seem no longer theirs but "exotic people's." One of Montag's earliest realizations in the novel is that his house is exactly like thousands of others. Identical and therefore capable of substitution, it can never be his own. That is why the clichéd designation by the media of Millie as "homemaker" is so absurdly ironic because at the very moment when the television is promoting one role it is also feeding her with desires which push in the opposite direction, ultimately inviting her to identify with another place preferable to her more mundane present house. *Fahrenheit 451* dramatizes the effects of the media as substitutions. Millie finds an ersatz intimacy with the "family" on the screen which contrasts markedly with her relation to Montag. Again and again the dark space of their bedroom is stressed, its coldness and silence; whereas Millie's favourite soap operas keep up a constant hubbub and medley of bright colours.

Millie and her friends are defined entirely by their roles as consumers, whether of sedatives, soap-operas, or fast cars. Bradbury anticipates Marshall McLuhan by presenting the media which stimulate this consumption as extensions of faculties (the thimble anticipations of Walkmans) or their substitutes (the toaster has hands to save her the trouble of touching the bread). . . . Mildred's house combines all the electronic gadgetry associated with the fifties "good life." But these things have a cost. Bradbury further anticipates McLuhan in rendering television as an aggressive medium: "Music bombarded him at such an immense volume that his bones were almost shaken from his tendons," and then, as it quietens down, "you had the impression that someone had turned on a washing-machine or sucked you up in a gigantic vacuum." The experience of one consumable can only be understood through comparison with another, and here the individual is put into a posture of maximum passivity as subjected to machines, not their controller. McLuhan explains the television in far more positive terms, but still ones which partly echo Bradbury's. Thus "with TV, the viewer is the screen. He is bombarded with light impulses." And because TV is no good for background it makes more demands on the viewer than does radio: "Because the low definition of TV insures a high degree of audience involvement, the most effective programs are those that present situations which consist of some process to be completed."[9] Bradbury burlesques this notion of audience participation as no more than an electronic trick whereby an individual's name can be inserted into a gap in the announcer's script (and even his lip-movements adjusted).

The media in Bradbury's novel then induce a kind of narcosis. There is both a continuity and an analogy between Millie watching the wall-screens and then taking sleeping pills. . . .

MONTAG'S FLIGHT

The essential trigger to [Montag's flight from his culture] is supplied by an alienation not only from suburban monotony but also from [his] consumer-wife. He contemplates her as if she has ceased to be a human being: ". . . he saw her without opening his eyes, her hair burnt by chemicals to a brittle straw, her eyes with a kind of cataract unseen but suspect far behind the pupils, the reddened pouting lips, the body as thin as a praying mantis from dieting, and her flesh like white bacon." Millie here fragments into disparate features transformed by dye, cosmetics or dieting. Instead of being the consumer she is now consumed by commercially induced processes. The passage points backwards to an original state which is no longer recoverable. . . . The adjective "reddened" only appears to suggest a physical state prior to make-up. Later in the novel when Millie flees from the house without lipstick her mouth is simply "gone," as if the adjective has grotesquely taken over actuality from its referent.

Montag clearly functions as a satirical means for Bradbury to question the impetus of consumerism and passages like the one just quoted estrange Montag from an environment he has been taking for granted. . . .

REGISTERING DISSATISFACTION

It is of course a truism that the dystopias of the fifties base themselves on the premise that dissatisfaction with the preva-

9. Marshall McLuhan, *Understanding Media: The Extensions of Man* (London: Routledge and Kegan Paul, 1964), 41.

lent regime will be registered sooner or later by their protagonists. In order to accelerate this process of realization some novelists use catalyst-figures whose role is to function as a productive irritant in the protagonist's consciousness. So Clarisse, the niece it turns out of Leonard Mead, fascinates and disturbs Montag because she seems wilfully to stand outside social norms. Neither child nor woman, she introduces herself as a social misfit ("I'm seventeen and I'm crazy") and challenges Montag to confront awkward questions such as whether he is happy. . . .

Clarisse and then later an English professor named Faber stimulate Montag towards overt resistance, whereas Beatty functions as antagonist. From a very early stage in the novel Montag internalizes Beatty's voice as a censorious or punitive force, the voice of the superego resisting taboo thoughts or actions. Every scene where Beatty figures then becomes charged with ambiguity as if he is accusing Montag of crimes. When the latter comes down with a "fever" Beatty visits him without being called, explaining that he could foresee what was going to happen. In a simulation of a doctor's visit Beatty tries to deindividualize Montag's problem as a typical case which will pass. If we visualize Montag being addressed on the one side by Beatty and on the other by Faber like a morality play, although the latter occupies the moral high ground, Beatty represents a far more sinister presence by his uncanny knack of predicting what Montag will think. . . .

The key progression in this process is a shift from the latent to the overt, from the implicit to the explicit. Montag discovers an inner voice which he has been suppressing and his previously unified self fractures into dissociations of mind from body and limb from limb: "His hands had been infected, and soon it would be his arms. He could feel the poison work up his wrists and into his elbows and his shoulders, and then the hump-over from shoulder-blade to shoulder-blade like a spark leaping a gap. His hands were ravenous. And his eyes were beginning to feel hunger. . . ." The metaphor of poison encodes Montag's dissidence within the ideology of a regime devoted to maintaining the so-called health of the body politic; but the displaced hunger of his other limbs suggests a desire that will take him out of that dominant ideology. We can see from this passage how the issue of authority pervades the very style of the novel. In his 1968 article "Death Warmed Over" Bradbury mounts a spirited defence of classic horror movies and fantasy fiction by contrasting two broad artistic, methods: the accumulation of fact and the use of symbolism. He condemns the former as being appropriate to another discipline altogether: "We have fallen into the hands of the scientists, the reality people, the data collectors." And he goes on to propose selective resonance as an alternative. "The symbolic acts, not the minuscule details of the act, are everything."[10] Retrospectively this article helps to explain the method of *Fahrenheit 451* which, like the other dystopias of the period, uses the dissatisfaction of one individual to reflect on the general inadequacies of a regime perceived as in some sense totalitarian. . . .

CONSEQUENCES OF ESTRANGEMENT

The last part of *Fahrenheit 451* traces out the consequences of Montag's estrangement from his society. His physical flight expresses in terms of action a disengagement which has already taken place in his mind. . . .

One critic has complained that the last section of Bradbury's novel is "vague in political detail" but the national references are clear and specific.[11] The hoboes gathered round their campfires and constantly moving on to avoid a threatening state authority recall the unemployed transients of the Depression (even the rusting railway line strengthens this echo). And the leader of the campers is named after the Granger Movement which flourished in the USA in the late 1860s and 1870s. This movement made a collective protest against the encroachments of large-scale capitalism and asserted the values of the local agrarian community. Its Declaration of Purposes asserted the aim "to labor for the good of our Order, our Country, and mankind"; and the movement set up reading programmes for farming families among other measures.[12] Although Montag rediscovers the communal space of the campsite and although the campers do possess contemporary technology, all the appeal of place and community lies in its appeal to the past. Personal memory and collective history blur together as the novel concludes with an attempted exercise in radical conservation which plays on the reader's own historical memory of a lost agrarian past.

10. Bradbury, "Death Warmed Over," *Playboy*, (Jan. 1968), 252. 11. Donald Watt, "*Fahrenheit 451* as Symbolic Dystopia," in M.H. Greenberg and Joseph D. Olander, eds., *Ray Bradbury* (Edinburgh: Paul Harris, 1980), 213. 12. Solon Justus Buck, *The Granger Movement* (Cambridge, Mass.: Harvard University Press, 1933), 64.

A Skillfully Drawn Conformist Hell

Kingsley Amis

The real horror in the push to conform in *Fahrenheit 451* is not simply that individuality can be suppressed, writes noted author Kingsley Amis. Even worse is the idea that there is something in many people that longs for such suppression. It is here that Bradbury shows the real danger of creating the hell of forced conformity. Amis, author of *Lucky Jim* and other novels, has been a devotee of science fiction since he discovered it at the age of twelve.

[One] unlikely reason for Ray Bradbury's fame is that, despite his regrettable tendency to dime-a-dozen sensitivity, he is a good writer, wider in range than any of his colleagues, capable of seeing life on another planet as something extraordinary instead of just challenging or horrific, ready to combine this with strongly held convictions. These last, at any rate, appear in his story "Usher II," which opens on Mars with the building of a residence after the prescription in Poe's story, great care having been taken to get the tarn "black and lurid" enough, the sedge satisfactorily "gray and ebon," etc. Inside, there are copper bats controlled by electronic beams, brass rats, robot skeletons, and phantoms. Soon the Investigator of Moral Climates, one Garrett, arrives and orders demolition, under the ordinances which have prohibited and destroyed all works of fantasy from Poe to *The Wizard of Oz,* while no films are allowed except remakes of Ernest Hemingway. There is time for one huge party, at which all the guests are members of the Society for the Prevention of Fantasy and are publicly murdered one after another by robot apes, bisected by pendulums, prematurely buried, and so on. Garrett himself is led into the catacombs by Stendahl, the owner, who mentions Amontillado

Adapted from Kingsley Amis, *New Maps of Hell: A Survey of Science Fiction* (New York: Harcourt Brace, 1960). Copyright © 1960 Kingsley Amis. Reprinted with the kind permission of Jonathan Clowes Ltd., London, on behalf of the Literary Estate of Sir Kingsley Amis.

and produces a mason's trowel without drawing any reaction from Garrett. The rest is soon told:

> "Garrett," said Stendahl, "do you know why I've done this to you? Because you burned Mr. Poe's books without really reading them. You took other people's advice that they needed burning. Otherwise you'd have realised what I was going to do to you when we came down here a moment ago. Ignorance is fatal, Mr. Garrett."
>
> Garrett was silent.
>
> "I want this to be perfect," said Stendahl, holding his lantern so its light penetrated in upon the slumped figure. "Jingle your bells softly." The bells rustled. "Now, if you'll please say, 'For the love of God, Montresor,' I might let you free."
>
> The man's face came up in the light. There was a hesitation. Then grotesquely the man said, "For the love of God, Montresor."
>
> "Ah," said Stendahl, eyes closed. He shoved the last brick into place and mortared it tight. "*Requiescat in pace*, dear friend."
>
> He hastened from the catacomb.

The suppression of fantasy, or of all books, is an aspect of the conformist society often mentioned by other writers, but with Bradbury it is a specialty. His novel *Fahrenheit 451*—supposedly the temperature at which book-paper ignites—extends and fills in the assumptions of "Usher II." The hero, Montag, is a fireman, which means that on receiving an alarm he and his colleagues pile on to the wagon and go off and burn somebody's house down, one with books in it, under the regulations of the Firemen of America, "established, 1790, to burn English-influenced books in the Colonies. First Fireman: Benjamin Franklin." In the expected central dialogue, the fire chief explains to Montag how it all came about:

> "Classics cut to fit fifteen-minute radio shows, then cut again to fill a two-minute book column, winding up at last as a ten- or twelve-line dictionary resume. I exaggerate, of course. The dictionaries were for reference. But many were those whose sole knowledge of *Hamlet* . . . was a one-page digest in a book that claimed: *now at last you can read all the classics; keep up with your neighbors.* Do you see? Out of the nursery into the college and back to the nursery; there's your intellectual pattern. . . . Life is immediate, the job counts, pleasure lies all about after work. . . . More sports for everyone, group spirit, fun, and you don't have to think, eh? . . . Authors, full of evil thoughts, lock up your typewriters. . . . We must be all alike. Not everyone born free and equal, as the Constitution says, but everyone *made* equal. Each man the image of every other; then all are happy, for there are no mountains to make them cower,

to judge themselves against. So! A book is a loaded gun in the house next door. Burn it. Take the shot from the weapon. . . . Ask yourself, What do we want in this country above all? People want to be happy, isn't that right? Haven't you heard it all your life? I want to be happy, people say. Well, aren't they? Don't we keep them moving, don't we give them fun? That's all we live for, isn't it? For pleasure, for titillation? And you must admit our culture provides plenty of these. . . . If you don't want a man unhappy politically, don't give him two sides to a question to worry him; give him one. Better yet, give him none. . . . Don't give [him] any slippery stuff like philosophy or sociology to tie things up with. That way lies melancholy."

One could offer plenty of objections to that, starting with the apparently small point that complacency about sociology, which Bradbury shares with his colleagues, is at least as bad as complacency about the tabloidisation of the classics, and that what we ought to want is less sociology, not more. Further, there is about Bradbury, as about those I might call the non-fiction holders of his point of view, a certain triumphant lugubriousness, a kind of proleptic *schadenfreude* (world copyright reserved), a relish not always distinguishable here from satisfaction in urging a case, but different from it, and recalling the relish with which are recounted the horrors of [George Orwell's] *Nineteen Eighty-Four* and a famous passage that prefigured it in *Coming Up for Air*. Jeremiah has never had much success in pretending he doesn't thoroughly enjoy his job, and whereas I agree with him, on the whole, in his dislike of those who reach for their revolver when they hear the word "culture," I myself am getting to the point where I reach for my ear-plugs on hearing the phrase "decline of our culture." But in this respect Bradbury sins no more grievously than his non-fiction colleagues, whom he certainly surpasses in immediacy, for *Fahrenheit 451* is a fast and scaring narrative, a virtue hard to illustrate by quotation. There are at least two good dramatic coups, one when a creature called the Mechanical Hound, constructed to hunt down book-owners and other heretics, looks up from its kennel in the fire station and growls at the hero, the other when Montag goes out on duty with the Salamander, as the fire engine is called, and finds that the alarm refers to his own house. The book emerges quite creditably from a comparison with *Nineteen Eighty-Four* as inferior in power, but superior in conciseness and objectivity. At the end, of course, Montag eludes the Mechanical Hound and joins a band of distinguished hoboes who are preserving the classics by learning them by heart.

Bradbury's is the most skilfully drawn of all science fiction's conformist hells. One invariable feature of them is that however activist they may be, however convinced that the individual can, and will, assert himself, their programme is always to resist or undo harmful change, not to promote useful change. . . . Thus to call the generic political stance of science fiction "radical," as I have done, is not quite precise: it is radical in attitude and temper, but strongly conservative in alignment.[1] This, however, does not weaken its claim to be regarded as, some of the time and in some sense, a literature of warning, as propaganda, not always unintelligent, against the notion that we can leave the experts to work things out for us. Such is equally the impression given, I think, by our next topic, utopias in which the forces of evil show themselves in economic and technological, rather than political, terms. . . . In the next section I shall show how Mrs. Montag amused herself while Montag was busy on his incendiary routine of "Monday . . . Millay, Wednesday Whitman, Friday Faulkner."

> Without turning on the light he imagined how this room would look. His wife stretched on the bed, uncovered and cold, like a body displayed on the lid of a tomb, her eyes fixed to the ceiling by invisible threads of steel, immovable. And in her ears the little seashells, the thimble radios tamped tight, and an electronic ocean of sound, of music and talk and music and talk coming in, coming in on the shore of her unsleeping mind. The room was indeed empty. Every night the waves came in and bore her off on their great tides of sound, floating her, wide-eyed, toward morning. There had been no night in the last two years that Mildred had not swum that sea, had not gladly gone down in it for the third time.

As regular readers will have guessed, Mildred is Mrs. Montag, wife of Ray Bradbury's book-burning fireman. It emerges, I think, that while it will not do for science fiction to characterize in conventional, differentiating terms, it can have something to say about human nature by dint of isolating and extending some observable tendency of behaviour, by showing, in this case, how far the devolution of individual-

---

1. "Negative" might be a better description. Such glimpses of the post-totalitarian future as we can glean show a society just like our own, but with more decency and less television. Nobody ever says how these reforms are to be brought about. Further, no positive utopias, dramatising schemes of political or other betterment, can be found in contemporary science fiction. Modern visionaries in general seem to have lost interest in any kind of social change, falling back on notions of self-salvation via naturopathy, orgonomy, or the psychic diagnostics of Edgar Cayce.

ity might go if the environment were to be modified in a direction favourable to this devolution. The lesson to be drawn from the more imaginative science-fiction hells, such as Bradbury's is not only that a society could be devised that would frustrate the active virtues, nor even that these could eventually be suppressed, but that there is in all sorts of people something that longs for this to happen. There are plenty of embryonic Mrs. Montags waiting for the chance to be wafted away by the Seashells,[2] or to share her jolly evenings at the Fun Park, breaking windows or smashing up cars with the steel ball, to join with her in watching three-wall television and trying to persuade her husband to get the fourth wall put in. This eager denial of mind, this longing to abandon reality via mechanical wonders, is obviously relevant to the political thesis of Bradbury's *Fahrenheit 451* and of many other works: the deliberate use of technology to promote an unworthy quiescence is a familiar idea. Correspondingly, Mildred Montag is a victim of epidemic neurosis: a cleverly staged scene shows her being brought round after a suicide attempt by a couple of cigarette-puffing handymen who just have time to use the almost fully automatic evacuation machine on her before rushing off to the next of their dozen nightly cases. What is most important here, however, is clearly the notion of the Seashell jag, for this need presuppose no kind of political manipulation, whether malevolent or mistakenly paternalistic.

Versions of the Seashells occur in the work of many writers primarily concerned to question unrestricted technological and commercial development. Often a novelty is envisaged which is not only more pleasurable than that reality which Mr. Eliot says we cannot bear very much of, but also as durable. There is actually no reason why Mildred Montag should ever have done anything else but listen to the Seashells, an idea taken to its logical conclusion in a delightfully nasty little story by John D. MacDonald, "Spectator Sport." A man who has been given a pre-frontal lobotomy by

2. Bradbury himself notes: *In writing the short novel "Fahrenheit 451," I thought I was describing a world that might evolve in four or five decades. But only a few weeks ago, in Beverly Hills one night, a husband and wife passed me, walking their dog. I stood staring after them, absolutely stunned. The woman held in one hand a small cigarette-package-sized radio, its antenna quivering. From this sprang tiny copper wires which ended in a dainty cone plugged into her right ear. There she was, oblivious to man and dog, listening to far winds and whispers and soap-opera cries, sleepwalking, helped up and down curbs by a husband who might just as well not have been there. This was not fiction.*

mistake is compensated by receiving for nothing what everybody else is saving up all his money for: total and irrevocable immersion in three-dimensional panaesthetic participatory television, the favourite series opted for being Western, Crime and Detection, and Harem. A pair of bored technicians, first cousins to Bradbury's antisuicide team, are hurrying around doing the requisite surgery on the day's quota. A variation on this theme takes the form of an admonitory satire on tranquillisers in Frederik Pohl's story "What to Do Till the Analyst Comes." After an unusually severe lung-cancer scare, the researchers come up with a chewing gum containing a euphoric drug that is not addictive, simply very agreeable. The whole world takes up Cheery-Gum, becoming totally happy and unneurotic and idle, secure in the knowledge that the stuff can be given up at any time, just as bridge-playing can. Only the hero is prevented by an allergy from joining in the universal merry-go-round.

Despite its lighthearted tone, what is at work in this story is obviously the same as that in "Spectator Sport" and Bradbury's Seashell episode: the fear of a pleasure so overmastering that it can break down the sense of reality, or at least the pattern of active life, and break them down in everyone, not merely in the predisposed neurotic. This feeling is not always treated thematically; it appears significantly often as background decoration, and I might almost have fitted it into my discussion of science fiction and the unconscious, were it not so conscious. In the preface to a collection containing one such story—the agent here is a melody, mathematically arrived at of course, which produces catatonic ecstasy—Arthur Clarke notes an article in the *Scientific American* for October, 1956; the subject: "Pleasure Centers in the Brain." It seems that the electrical stimulation of a certain part of a rat's brain causes the animal intense pleasure. When the rat finds it can stimulate itself for a second or so by pressing a lever, it spends most of its time doing this.

> Electric stimulation in some of these regions actually appeared to be far more rewarding to the animals than an ordinary satisfier such as food. For example, hungry rats ran faster to reach an electric stimulator than they did to reach food. Indeed, a hungry animal often ignored available food in favor of the pleasure of stimulating itself electrically. Some rats . . . stimulated their brains more than 2,000 times per hour for 24 consecutive hours! . . . Enough of the brain-

stimulating work has been repeated on monkeys . . . to indicate that our general conclusions can very likely be gener-
alised eventually to human beings—with modifications, of
course.

I cannot say that I feel more frightened by that than by any
crisis in Berlin or around Formosa, but I think perhaps I
should.

Literature—and the Literate—Will Prevail

Susan Spencer

Susan Spencer notes that some ancient Greeks were suspicious of writing: it was technology, and it threatened the personal role of the storyteller in interpreting a tale. Modern writers, on the other hand, assume that writing is here to stay, but Bradbury's book warns against what can happen when a culture turns against the idea of literacy. Although the books seems to come full circle to the idea of an oral storytelling tradition, the people-books Montag joins at the end of *Fahrenheit 451* are merely "holding" their texts until it is once again safe to commit them to paper. Susan Spencer is an instructor in the Department of English at the University of Central Oklahoma.

At the dawn of widespread literacy in fourth-century Athens, Plato appended to the end of his *Phaedrus* a story that has often been perceived as, as Jacques Derrida puts it, "an extraneous mythological fantasy." Derrida argues in *Dissemination* that there is nothing extraneous about the myth at all, but rather it is an expression of an important and timely idea with which the classical Athenians were concerned. Recent orality/literacy theory, as outlined by Eric A. Havelock, Walter S. Ong, and others, would seem to back him up. The story is that of the discovery of the technology of writing, a tale that Socrates claims is traditional among the Egyptians. According to Socrates, the god Theuth invented this technology and offered it to the king of Upper Egypt as something that would "make the people of Egypt wiser and improve their memories" (*Phaedrus* 274b). But the king scorned Theuth's gift, saying:

> by reason of your tender regard for the writing that is your offspring, [you] have declared the very opposite of its true ef-

Excerpted from Susan Spencer, "The Post-Apocalyptic Library: Oral and Literate Culture in *Fahrenheit 451* and *A Canticle for Leibowitz*," *Extrapolation*, vol. 32, no. 4 (Winter 1991), pp. 331–42. Reprinted by permission of The Kent State University Press. (References cited in the original have been omitted in this reprint.)

fect. If men learn this, it will implant forgetfulness in their souls; they will cease to exercise memory because they rely on that which is written, calling things to remembrance no longer from within themselves, but by means of external marks. What you have discovered is a recipe not for memory, but for reminder. And it is no true wisdom that you offer your disciples, but only its semblance, for by telling them of many things without teaching them you will make them seem to know much, while for the most part they know nothing, and as men filled, not with wisdom, but with the conceit of wisdom, they will be a burden to their fellows. (275a,b)

TELLING WITHOUT TEACHING

The remark about "telling them . . . without teaching them" is evidently an expression of uneasiness with the idea of text as what Ong calls "unresponsive." In *Orality and Literacy: The Technologizing of the Word*, Ong sees one of Socrates's arguments as being "if you ask a person to explain his or her statement, you can get an explanation; if you ask a text, you get back nothing except the same, often stupid, words which called for your question in the first place." While this idea is so commonplace to us as to go practically unnoticed, except when we are frustrated by a particularly opaque text, it was new and frightening to the Greeks. According to Havelock in "The Oral Composition of Greek Drama" (*Literate Revolution* 261–312), the late fifth and early fourth century B.C. was a period of relatively rapid change in literary style, as a direct result of the spread of popular literacy. Not only was an explanatory oral framework done away with, but also the old formulaic devices that helped oral composers keep their place and remember what they were talking about. "Compositionally, as plays began to be written with the expectation of being read, the composer would feel a reduced pressure to conform to certain mnemonic rules. The invented would be freer to prevail over the expected." This, Havelock hypothesizes, created some tension in the Greek theater—a tension that can be traced in Aristophanes's *Frogs*, where the more conservative, more "oral" Aeschylus wins a contest against the more "literary" and startlingly original Euripides; and, as we can see (although Havelock does not mention it here), in the inherent uneasiness in Plato's *Phaedrus*.

Although "The Oral Composition of Greek Drama" was first published in 1980, some theory of postliterary tension was working its way into the intelligentsia several decades before. To quote Havelock again, in his 1950 book *The Crucifixion of Intellectual Man,* the myth of the Fall in Genesis, as a direct result of eating of the tree of knowledge, "gives poignant expression to that conflict within the civilized consciousness of man, between his sense of intellectual power and his distrust and fear of that power. . . . All the warmth and the richness of man's nature demand that he live in the protection of certain illusions in order to be secure, happy, and peaceful." The "expected" rather than the "invented." The further the artificial "memory" created by textuality stretches back, and the more it can be built upon by an advancing science, the more that security fades away. Man becomes dangerous and also frightened. "Though our science may kill us, it will never allow us to retreat. Somehow we know that we would never burn enough books, nor eliminate enough intellectuals, to be able to return to the warm room" of blissful ignorance.

FAHRENHEIT 451

Within a decade of this assurance, two famous science fiction novels appeared dealing with the very attempt that Havelock had just pronounced futile: Ray Bradbury's *Fahrenheit 451* (1953) and Walter M. Miller's *A Canticle for Leibowitz* (1959). In *Fahrenheit 451* the protagonist, Guy Montag, is a "fireman"; that is, he burns forbidden books, and the houses that hide them, for a living. This is a busy job, considering the fact that just about all books are forbidden. There are a few rare exceptions, such as three-dimensional comic books, trade journals and, of course, rule books, those mainstays of any oppressive society. The rule book for the Firemen of America includes a brief history of the profession: "Established 1790, to burn English-influenced books in the Colonies. First Fireman: Benjamin Franklin." According to the only available text, and to the voice of political authority, this is a glorious and time-honored profession, an idea that gives the firemen a sense of continuity and security . . . and, perhaps, allows Bradbury to make a comment on the fact that textual knowledge is power, even—or perhaps especially—false knowledge. Power becomes unbreachable if textual information is monolithic. According to the sinister but brilliant fire chief, Beatty, the main danger in books is that "none of those books agree with each other." Very true, but a danger to whom? Peace of mind, he argues repeatedly. To one law-

breaker, kneeling despairingly amid her kerosene-soaked illegal books, Beatty cries, "You've been locked up here for
years with a regular damned Tower of Babel. Snap out of it!"

Inevitably, Montag becomes discontented with the status
quo and curious about this nebulous "danger." Both his dis-
content and his curiosity are intensified when the woman
mentioned above chooses to burn with her books rather
than lose them. Beatty, seeing his distress when Montag
feels "sick" and feigns illness, explains the real advent of the
firemen in phrases that echo Havelock's concept of the loss
of the "warm room" but takes it to its extreme limit:

> You always dread the unfamiliar. . . . We must all be alike. Not
> everyone born free and equal, as the Constitution says, but
> everyone *made* equal. Each man the image of every other;
> then all are happy, for there are no mountains to make them
> cower, to judge themselves against.

On the literary side, he also echoes Plato on the "conceit of
wisdom," and just how far that can be taken as a sort of leveling device:

> Give the people contests they win by remembering the words
> to more popular songs or the names of state capitals or how
> much corn Iowa grew last year. Cram them full of noncom-
> bustible data, chock them so damned full of "facts" they feel
> stuffed, but absolutely "brilliant" with information. Then
> they'll feel they're thinking, they'll get a *sense* of motion with-
> out moving. And they'll be happy, because facts of that sort
> don't change. Don't give them any slippery stuff like philoso-
> phy or sociology to tie things up with. That way lies melan-
> choly.

These things are written, but they are not literature. The
classicist may be reminded here of the problems associated
with Linear B, the proto-Greek script found at Mycenae and
Knossos. All of the inscriptions are "bald counting-house
dockets," (Palmer 13), "a text of the greatest interest" being
a tablet that "lists amounts of barley against various classes
of craftsmen" (Palmer 104). There is no literature *per se*, un-
less one were to use the standard eighteenth-century definition of literature as "anything written." As a result, it is difficult to get students interested in learning Linear B. There
is simply nothing interesting to read. The situation is described by Havelock as one of preliteracy, in spite of the
physical existence of written text: "whereas historians who
have touched upon literacy as a historical phenomenon have
commonly measured its progress in terms of the history of

writing, the actual conditions of literacy depend upon the history not of writing but of reading" (*Literate Revolution* 56). One needs an audience. Get the audience to lose interest, and you can do away with the literate civilization. In *Fahrenheit 451* the reader has the feeling of moving backward in time to a preliterate society, and the content of the society's "literature," although here it is for political ends, strengthens this impression.

The last phrase of Beatty's pronouncement, "That way lies melancholy," with its literary overtones—very different from the plainer common speech of his subordinates—is not unusual for Beatty. In keeping with the idea that knowledge is power, Bradbury gives us several hints that the fire chief has had frequent access to the forbidden texts and that this is either

---

THE POWER OF AMERICAN SOCIETY

Fahrenheit 451 *offers a warning about the dangers of book burning in any country, in any era—but the author believes in America's ability to pull itself back from the edge of destruction.*

"When I wrote my novel *Fahrenheit 451* during the years from 1949 to 1953, we were living at the heart of what is known now as the McCarthy era. We were very close to panic and wholesale bookburning. I never believed we would go all out and destroy ourselves in this fashion. I have always believed in the power of our American society to rectify error without having to resort to destruction. Sometimes it takes a long time to swing the pendulum back in the direction of sanity. But the pendulum did swing. McCarthy *is* dead, and the era that carried his name buried with him.

"Still," Mr. Bradbury added, "I feel that what I had to say in *Fahrenheit 451* is valid today and will continue to be valid here and in other countries in other years.". . .

Mr. Bradbury adds, in passing, that the Russians, thinking he had written an exclusive criticism of McCarthyism in the U.S.A., pirated *Fahrenheit 451* a few years ago. Published and sold in an edition of some 500,000 copies, the authorities suddenly discovered he meant tyranny over the mind at any time or place.

"In sum," he says: "Russia, too. The novel has now gone underground, I hear. Which makes me, I gather, the *clean* Henry Miller of the Soviets."

Ray Bradbury, quoted in *ALA Bulletin*, May 1961.

a cause or a result of his being made chief (just which one is unclear). Like Kurt Vonnegut, Jr.'s short story "Harrison Bergeron," set in another disturbing dystopia where "everybody [is] finally equal," some people are seen clearly to be more equal than others and thus enabled to wield power over their fellows. In Vonnegut's story, the ascendancy is physical: Diana Moon Glampers, the "Handicapper General," is the only citizen who isn't decked out in distorting glasses, distracting ear transmitters, and bags of birdshot to weaken her to the level of society's lowest common denominator. In *Fahrenheit 451*, the ascendancy is purely textual, but that is enough. Beatty's obnoxious confidence and habit of quoting famous works strikes the reader immediately and leads to a question that Bradbury never answers: why is this highly literate person permitted to survive, let alone hold a position of high authority, in an aggressively oral society? Something is rotten in the whole system. Evidently someone higher up, Beatty's shadowy superior, feels that there is some inherent value in a well-read man, in spite of all the political rhetoric. This probability is directly opposed to Beatty's frequent deprecation of texts (a protection of his own monopoly?) and claim that the eventual ban of almost all books was not a political coup accomplished by a power-hungry elite at one fell swoop. Beatty's explanation, which we are never called upon to doubt, is that an outraged people seeking complete equality called for more and more censorship as texts became more widely available to interest groups that might be offended by them: "It didn't come from the Government down. There was no dictum, no declaration, no censorship, to start with, no! Technology, mass exploitation, and minority pressure carried the trick." As Plato warned thousands of years earlier, well-read man had become an offensive "burden to his fellows."

Bradbury closes the novel, however, with an optimistic view: the text *will* prevail, and man will be the better for it. This is shown symbolically in the escape from the city by Montag and Faber, the only two literate men in the story besides Beatty—who, also symbolically, perishes in the same manner as the many books he has burned. The ignorant oral-culture citizens, radios tamped securely in their ears, remain in the city to be blown up by an enemy they could easily have escaped, if it weren't for the fact that their monolithic media preferred to keep them ignorant and happy. Having taken up with a group of itinerant professors, haltingly trying to remember the text of

Ecclesiastes, Montag takes the first steps toward realizing the dream he had as he blindly fled the government's persecution: "Somewhere the saving and the putting away had to begin again and someone had to do the saving and keeping, one way or another, in books, in records, in people's heads, any way at all so long as it was safe, free from moths, silverfish, rust and dry-rot, and men with matches."[1]

The idea that it is safe only when locked away in memory is almost a startling one in this book that so privileges the literary text; it seems as if the author has come full circle to an oral culture and the need to circumvent the shortcomings of Theuth's invention. Yet Bradbury makes it clear that they will write everything down as soon as possible and will try to reconstruct a fully literate society again. This should not take long, and is certainly desirable. The concept of text is a progressive thing, not a cyclical, and as long as any remnants remain there is always a base, however small, on which to build a better and wiser world.

Works Cited

Bradbury, Ray. *Fahrenheit 451*. New York: Ballantine, 1979.

Derrida, Jacques. *Dissemination*. Trans. Barbara Johnson. Chicago: U of Chicago P, 1981.

Havelock, Eric A. *The Literate Revolution in Greece and Its Cultural Consequences*. Princeton, NJ: Princeton UP, 1982.

———, *The Crucifixion of Intellectual Man*. Boston: Beacon Press, 1951.

Miller, Walter M., Jr. *A Canticle for Leibowitz*. London: Black Swan, 1984.

Ong, Walter S. *Orality and Literacy: The Technologizing of the Word*. New York: Methuen, 1982.

Palmer, Leonard R. *Myceneans and Minoans: Aegean Prehistory in the Light of the Linear B Tablets*. New York: Knopf, 1962.

Plato, *Phaedrus*. Trans. R. Hackforth. *Plato: Collected Dialogues*. Ed. Edith Hamilton and Huntington Cairns. Princeton, NJ: Princeton UP, 1961.

Vonnegut, Kurt, Jr. "Harrison Bergeron." *Welcome to the Monkey House*. New York: Dell, 1970. 7–13.

---

1. This, of course, is a Biblical echo: "Lay up for yourselves treasures in heaven, where neither moth nor rust doth corrupt, and where thieves do not break through nor steal" (Matthew 6:20).

Can Books Convert Dystopia into Utopia?

John Huntington

The urban world at the beginning of *Fahrenheit 451*
is a dystopia, a dehumanizing environment, as John
Huntington observes, where the state keeps citizens
in thrall by denying them the kinds of positive, useful intellectual stimuli found in books. The novel
urges that books—a symbol of old, positive values—
must be preserved to prevent the horrors of this
mindless future. Yet, Huntington points out, this argument becomes ambiguous at the end of the novel,
when the book-people's leader declares that books
had not made life better even when they were freely
available in the past. Huntington teaches in the English Department of the University of Illinois,
Chicago Circle.

Darko Suvin defines *utopia* as "a verbal construction of a particular quasi-human community where sociopolitical institu-
tions, norms, and individual relationships are organized according to a more perfect principle than in the author's
community." Suvin is especially concerned with seeing
utopia as a *literary* form. Accepting that, I want here also to
stress the importance of *organization, community*, and *principle* in this definition. The utopia is an exercise in thinking
through a way things might fit together, might work; it strives
for consistency and reconciles conflict. . . .

Dystopia, in the structural configuration I am here defining, is similar to utopia. Dystopia (the bad place) is for our
purposes utopia in which the positive ("more perfect principle") has been replaced by a negative. Though opposites on
the surface, utopia and dystopia share a common structure:
both are exercises in imagining coherent wholes, in making
an idea work, either to lure the reader towards an ideal or to

drive the reader back from a nightmare. Both are the expression of a synthetic imagination, a comprehension and expression of the deep principles of happiness or unhappiness.

By *anti-utopia* I propose to refer to a type of skeptical imagining that is opposed to the consistencies of utopia-dystopia. If the utopian-dystopian form tends to construct single, fool-proof structures which solve social dilemmas, the anti-utopian form discovers problems, raises questions, and doubts. . . . Anti-utopia, as I am here defining it, . . . is a mode of relentless inquisition, of restless skeptical exploration of the very articles of faith on which utopias themselves are built. Thus, while there is much anti-utopian satire, it is not an attack on reality but an exploration of conflicts in human desire and expectation. . . .

TRANSFORMING DYSTOPIA INTO UTOPIA

To transform . . . a dystopia into utopia requires discovering a different set of images that will be similarly free from ambiguity and conflict but which will function positively instead of negatively. Positive and negative are deceptive terms here; they imply a symmetry around a neutral middle which is in fact very difficult to achieve. It is a commonplace of modern criticism that there are no authentic heroes, only anti-heroes. Whereas the purely negative image is easily acceded to, the positive is deeply suspect. A single negative connotation will rob an image of its positive value, while a single positive connotation will not prevent an image from seeming totally negative. To say that a rat is intelligent does not make it any the less powerfully negative; like Satan, "by merit raised/To that bad eminence," its virtues simply increase its horror. On the other hand, positive images can be rendered ineffectual by a simple observation of how powerless they are. Given this imbalance in the present state of values, the utopian image must often depend on what in cinematic terms we would call soft-focus: a blurred vision which never looks closely enough at the image to discover flaws. . . . We see such a blur at the heart of Ray Bradbury's *Fahrenheit 451*.

Montag, the protagonist of Bradbury's novel, . . . is a man coming to consciousness and attempting the overthrow or reformation of the closed, totalitarian, futuristic world he valued at the start. . . . A woman is the inspiration for the change of mind. As in other works, the act of seeing beyond the present is at least in part an act of recovery of a lost tradition: . . . Montag rediscovers books, which the future society has banned. . . .

In *Fahrenheit 451* the future is bad because people, denied the rich traditional culture contained in books and imaged by nature, have become unstimulated and unstimulating. The dystopian world is in large part conveyed in terms of the denial of positives. Firechief Beatty's defense of the bookless future is essentially that of the Grand Inquisitor, with the important change that the mass's fear of freedom is seen to be a historical phenomenon, a failure of education. In the past, so the ironic argument goes, people were capable of freedom, but because of technology and the triumph of a debased mass culture they

---

THE IMPORTANCE OF BOOKS

English teacher Charles F. Hamblen discusses how his students discovered Bradbury's central point.

The nucleus of the book . . . is the scene in which Captain Beatty, Montag's ironically paternal superior, explains the evolution of their society to his wavering henchman. . . . To parallel the rapid pace of twentieth-century life, books were condensed, first to digests, ultimately to dictionary resumés. Reflective thought was virtually eliminated. . . .What books and magazines did survive were completely watered down to avoid the rancor of vociferous minorities. Automation completed the trek to total non-intellectuality. Censorship was almost an afterthought, merely established to stifle those few, stubborn, philosophical souls who occasionally cropped up.

As he finishes his bravura performance, Beatty sums up the fireman's position:

> The important thing for you to remember, Montag, is we're The Happiness Boys, The Dixie Duo, you and I and the others. We stand against the small tide of those who want to make everyone unhappy with conflicting theory and thought. We have our fingers in the dike. Hold steady. Don't let the torrent of melancholy and drear philosophy drown our world. We depend on you. I don't think you realize how important *you* are, *we* are, to our happy world as it stands now.

This is Bradbury at his satirical, hard-hitting best and it effectively structured the students' thinking about the rest of the book. They could see why, in that terrible, antiseptic time, rocking chairs and front porches were abolished, why people talked but didn't *say* anything, why the human soul atrophied, and why Beatty indirectly committed suicide. And most significantly, they saw why books are important.

Charles F. Hamblen, "Bradbury's *Fahrenheit 451* in the Classroom," *English Journal*, September 1968.

have lost their ability to choose and their joy in freedom.

Beatty's argument seems to be the author's; in Montag's wife we see heavily done exactly the mindlessness, the need for booklessness that Beatty defends. Beatty argues that mass culture is necessarily simple and, therefore, inevitably a decline from our own élite culture based on books, and in much of its satire the novel supports him. Where the novel makes Beatty clearly an ironic spokesman to be refuted is not in his characterization of the masses and what they want, but in his inadequate appreciation of the sensitive few who are capable of freedom.

The novel expresses this vision of freedom with images of sentimentalized nature (Clarisse rhapsodizes about the smell of leaves, the sight of the man in the moon), the recollection of the small, mid-western town (the front porch and the rocking chair become symbols of freedom), some tag ends of 1930s' romanticizing of Depression survival, and an unquestioning admiration for books. This cluster poses an absolute pole around which accrues all good and in relation to which all movement away is bad. The dystopian and utopian possibilities in the novel are thus represented by separate clusters of images and ideas that the novel finds unambiguous and leaves unchallenged.

IGNORED IMPLICATIONS

What needs emphasis here is the extent to which Bradbury's novel preserves the dystopian-utopian structure by ignoring the implications of its own imagery. The author advises his audience that they must preserve books to prevent the horror he imagines, but he never questions the values implicit in the books. When the new age is accused of serious flaws—unhappiness, fear, war, and wasted lives—there is no sense that the age of books may have also suffered from such problems. At the end, in his vision of a wandering group of book-people Bradbury invokes an idealized hobo mystique, but with little sense of the limits and tragedy of such a life.

[In such a simple system of good and bad values, mediation produces horror rather than thought. Nature is good and technology is bad, but the ultimate terror is a mixture of the two, a kind of symbolic miscegenation.] When Montag finally makes his break from the technological future he is pursued by a "mechanical hound," a terrifying figure which combines the relentlessness of the bloodhound with the infallibility of technology. In Bradbury's vision the hound is most terrifying for being both alive and not alive.

The threat the hound poses for the imagery system of the novel is put to rest the moment Montag escapes him, and the clear opposition between technology and nature that Clarisse has preached strongly reasserts itself. Montag hears a whisper, sees "a shape, two eyes" in the forest and is convinced it is the hound, but it turns out to be a deer, not just harmless, but afraid of him. Nature is submissive and controllable, while technology is predatory and threatening. This important refuge then leads to a sequence of reversals. Montag sees a fire in the woods and for the first time in his life realizes that fire need not be destructive, that in providing warmth it can be benign. And this perception leads to a moment of trance in which Montag resees himself:

> How long he stood he did not know, but there was a foolish and yet delicious sense of knowing himself as an animal come from the forest, drawn by the fire. He was a thing of brush and liquid eye, of fur and muzzle and hoof, he was a thing of horn and blood that would smell like autumn if you bled it out on the ground.

I take it that this reduction of the human to animal parts is somehow consoling and ennobling. Like all the nature images in this novel, the purple rhetoric obscures true perception, but nevertheless the revelation is there and the blurred but central symbolic transformation of the novel is complete: Montag has escaped the urban world of destructive technology and joined the nurturing forest world. By rescuing fire for the good, natural side, he has enabled the novel to convert dystopia into utopia.

WHERE DO BOOKS FIT IN?

The interesting difficulty is where do books fit into this simple opposition? Since Gutenberg the book has been a symbol of technological progress. Bradbury partly counters this meaning of his symbol by reducing his pastoral, not to paper books, but to humans who remember books. Thus the replication and general availability that are books' virtues, but which the novel has seen as the instruments of the mass-culture that has ruined the world, are denied. We have the *idea* of the book without the *fact* of its production. Then, by becoming a general symbol of the past now denied, the book becomes a symbol for all old values, but this symbolism brings up two difficulties. First, whatever good books have propagated, they have also preached the evils that have oppressed the world. The very technology that the novel finds threatening would be impossible without books. Second, books can readily inspire a repressive and tradition-bound pedantry which, while anti-technological, is also against nature.

Through most of *Fahrenheit 451* Bradbury simply ignores these potential problems with his symbol; but in the final pages, in an act of renunciation that is surprising given the values the novel has promulgated, the moral vision retreats from its main symbolism. The memorizers of books are about to move out of the forest to give succor to the cities that have just been bombed; and Granger, the leader of the bookish hoboes, says:

> Hold onto one thought: you're not important. You're not anything. Some day the load we're carrying with us may help someone. But even when we had the books on hand, a long time ago, we didn't use what we got out of them. We went right on insulting the dead. We went right on spitting on the graves of all the poor ones who died before us. We're going to meet a lot of lonely people in the next week and the next month and the next year. And when they ask us what we're doing, you can say, We're remembering. That's where we'll win out in the long run. And some day we'll remember so much that we'll build the biggest steamshovel in history and dig the biggest grave of all time and shove war in and cover it up.

The vagueness, ambiguity, and misdirection of this passage confuse what Granger is saying; but in the technological imagery of the last line and in the attack on the previously sentimentalized past, in the recognition that books have done little to make life better, this paragraph implies a renunciation of the values the novel has been, however naïvely, building. But perhaps it is also, finally, an awareness of a true opposition, of an irony that gets beyond the simple sentimentalisms of much of the novel. Though one may have doubts as to how to take it, one way would be to see here a titanic revision of values, a deep questioning of the pieties that have inspired Montag and Clarisse. In line with such a reading we should observe that one of the books Montag remembers is *Ecclesiastes:* perhaps this is an allusion to the Preacher's famous words against the vanity of life, and particularly the vanity of books. But, then, to read it this way would be to suppose that Bradbury is attempting anti-utopian thought, and that seems unlikely. . . . Bradbury's novel is clearly utopian-dystopian.

Overcoming Nihilism in the Modern World

William F. Touponce

Although *Fahrenheit 451* can be read as a critique of mass culture, William F. Touponce suggests a deeper, more personal metaphor. In comparing Bradbury's work to the nihilist writings of nineteenth-century German philosopher and existentialist Friedrich Nietzsche, Touponce interprets the novel as the story of the hero's journey through the modern "disease" of nihilism. Touponce is the author of two books on Bradbury: *Ray Bradbury*, from which this essay is excerpted, and *Ray Bradbury and the Poetics of Reverie*.

Fahrenheit 451 is definitely science fictional in intent. A central feature of the book, however, is the way in which it plays with contemporary utopian longings, . . . accomplishing nothing less than a revision in the very form and essence of the way in which those desires are conceived. Utopia conceived of as the fulfillment of a void in man, who then ceases to will, is rejected. The familiar utopian ideal of happiness for the greatest number is, I think, also rejected by the book, which finds the idea of the modern State just another source of seeming authority demanded from the outside. . . . It is a question of desiring things in another way entirely. In Bradbury's utopian society, the individual would desire only from plenitude of the will, and the novel ends by affirming the eternal recurrence of the utopian ideal which rises, like the phoenix, from the flames of man's self-destructive nihilism.

We may have difficulty in trying to decide the utopian logic of the novel in a first reading. We do not know, in short, whether Bradbury stands with those who believe in rational enlightenment and the critique of prejudices, wanting to expose the distortions of communication brought about by hidden violence and domination, or with those who romantically

Excerpted from William F. Touponce, *Ray Bradbury* (Mercer Island, WA: Starmont House, 1989). Reprinted by permission of the author. (Endnotes in the original have been omitted in this reprint.)

affirm the authority of tradition and myth. On the one hand, the book *is* a critique of mass culture, which it sees as oppressive with its constant stimulation of pseudo-needs, its creation of desire as lack in its victims (the main target is advertising, which it subjects to a Freudian critique). This tendency can only culminate in the reduction of all higher values to a "paste pudding norm," as Fire Chief Beatty, the defender of the *status quo*, succinctly puts it. On the other hand, Bradbury seems to realize, along with Nietzsche, that although the process of enlightenment made by science is critical, the critical dissolution of dogmas produces not liberation but indifference. It is not emancipatory, but nihilistic. Myths are also necessary for a healthy culture as well. My previous reading of this book traces what I took to be a negative dialectic of enlightenment that constantly puts the reader in a contradictory situation to bring out neglected states of mind. Perhaps this reading emphasizes too much the cognitive aspects of the book (See my *Ray Bradbury and the Poetics of Reverie*). If that is so, I would like now to balance that reading with an account of what may be a critique of critique, or at least an attempt to weigh the claims of a mythical past (in the form of literature) against a future of rational utopias, in some of the discussion which follows.

THE DISEASE OF NIHILISM

The book takes the form of a three-part "diagnosis" of the disease of modern man known as nihilism, in its complete and incomplete varieties. The first part shows the hero becoming sick, the second part deals with his rebellion and search for an antidote, and the third with a revaluation of values in which we learn the true value of the values put forth in the second part. Thus, there is in a sense a gradual process of enlightenment in the book and, at the same time, a revaluation of the book's earlier values. Yet the book is not anti-utopian, for as I have indicated, it ends by affirming the utopian ideal (actually in *allegory*, and not in myth, which is why we know that the book still maintains a critical stance against romanticism). . . . My use of medical terminology of sickness and health is consonant with Bradbury's own in the novel, . . . and not just a borrowing of Nietzsche's critical terminology, where such metaphors are prominent also. Indeed, there is an important thematic code in the book that organizes poisons, antidotes, infections and cures, pain-killers and stimulants, particularly with regard to the human bloodstream (as instinctive knowledge) and the stomach (as the capacity to digest or incorporate alien elements), which doubles as an indicator of moral strength, health, and sanity.

Once "infected" with the fever to read the books he normally burns, Montag the fireman is led on a search to find the origin of his unhappiness, and his search leads him through certain stages of nihilism. . . . However paradoxical it may sound to say this at the outset of our discussion, what Montag discovers is that his goal of enlightenment includes a reversal of itself; that is, there should be a limit on enlightenment. True happiness can only proceed from this understanding, and it is not a goal towards which we strive. Montag realizes that total science as an ideal leads to nihilism just as surely as Christian otherworldliness does, as Nietzsche knew. And any attempt to escape nihilism (understood here in the sense of the negation of the will to live) with reevaluating values simply produces the opposite, making the problem worse. Passing through pessimism, Montag at the end learns wisdom—what Nietzsche called the meaning of the earth—and thereby how to set the limits of knowledge at what can be made instinctive, part of a bodily self.

The philosophical position reached at the end, when Montag is living among a group of nomadic book-people, is best described as a determination to admit the necessity of constant revaluation to ourselves without any reservation and to stop telling ourselves tales in the old way. Hence, the sense of pathos we feel in some of the speeches made by Granger, the spokesman of the itinerant book-people, impels us to seek *new values*, not necessarily defined but nonetheless adumbrated by the novel itself. We learn that the world might be more valuable than we used to believe; we must see through the human tendency to make ideals fixed and eternal as a denial of life and becoming. While we thought that we accorded the world the highest interpretation and value (our readerly experience in Part Two), we actually may not have given our existence even a moderately fair value. . . .

In the [book's] opening scene the landscape of this fantastic world is infested with a poisonous mythical monster, the Salamander (fire engine) with its hose, described as a "great python spitting its venomous kerosene upon the world." We meet Montag, the agent of this poisoning, whose job it is to burn books which contain the memory of the past, the record of what different men and women have said and done throughout history, and therefore of anything which might contradict the State's will to truth, i.e., that everything should be reduced to the thinkable in terms of mass norms (what Beatty in his own unwittingly ironic way calls "noncombustible data," the facts of positivism that are supposed to make the people of this society feel brilliant without the need for interpretation). At the outset Montag is close to being a pyromaniac. He presides over a debased ritual that provides a carnival for the mass media to televise. Essentially, his nighttime job is entertainment in a society of spectacles, and he thoroughly identifies with it. The poisonous kerosene is perfume to him; a permanent fiery smile grips his face like a mask; he winks at himself in the fire station mirror, his face burnt black, a minstrel man.

Clarisse *vs.* Mildred

However, when Montag meets his teen-age neighbor, Clarisse, things begin to change. She has an impish sense of humor unknown to Montag (her "insanity" as she calls it) and little overt respect for the uniform he wears and its emblems of authority. Her constant wonder and curiosity, her intense *aliveness*, wakens Montag to a (largely natural) world outside his ego's identification with its social role. Her oneiric [pertaining to dreams] function is to activate the dreaming pole of Montag's consciousness, long repressed by this technological society. But her observations are also critical. She tells Montag, for example, that her education consists of "a lot of funnels and a lot of water poured down the spout and out the bottom, and them telling us it's wine when it's not." Wine will be a symbol of health in this novel, as elsewhere in Bradbury. Clarisse diagnoses Montag with a dandelion flower, revealing to him that he really does not love anyone. She also tells him about a fireman who committed suicide by setting a mechanical hound against himself, the hound being one of the most overcoded bearers of the health/sickness distinction. It is an uncanny embodiment of our existential problems which we have tried to banish by means of technology, yet it has come home, "full of poison wildness, of insanity and nightmare"; it murders its victims with a numbing dose of procaine. Because of her healthy family environment (which includes, according to her, being spanked when she needed it), she has been able to resist. It is she who "infects" Montag with the desire to read the books he burns and, therefore, with the need to regain his psychic health.

Montag's wife, Mildred, is the opposite of Clarisse. She embodies just about every form of self-narcotization available in this society and just about every way of avoiding the will to live and its affirmations. Deep down she is empty, suicidal, and she attempts to get over this by various forms of artificial intoxication: as music, she keeps a miniature radio tamped in her ear at all times (she communicates with Montag by lip-reading, training in such a skill having been thoughtfully supplied by the Sea Shell company); as cruelty, she drives her car down the highways at tremendous rates of speed, hoping to kill an animal (or better yet, a human being); and as a blind narcissistic enthusiasm for identifying with "exotic people's" lives, she wants most of all to buy another telescreen for their house, a fourth wall, to "make the dream complete." In appearance she is thin as a praying mantis from dieting, her hair burnt to a brittle straw by dyeing, her flesh described as the color of white bacon. Not a healthy type to be sure. She is a victim of mass culture and advertising that define desire as a lack and the subject (Mildred) as someone whose desires can never be fulfilled. On the same night as that of the book's opening conflagration, she attempts suicide by taking an overdose of sleeping pills and is later restored to "health" by an antisuicide team and its machine, which fills her bloodstream with the blood of a stranger. After this experience, Montag's faith in his marriage is profoundly shaken. He wonders whether he really knows this rosy-cheeked woman, or she him. He goes to sleep himself by taking a pill, saying that he does not know anything anymore.

ALIENATION

This is the first stage of disorientation associated with nihilism. The second phase begins with Montag's growing alienation from his job, an alienation which is made complete after an incident in which an old woman chooses to die in the fire that destroys her house and hidden library rather than be taken to the insane asylum. While looting the house, Montag is seized with an uncontrollable desire to steal a book for himself after a falling book accidentally lights on his hand exposing its beautiful snowy pages painted with words. In the brief moment, Montag is able to read one line of the book (which may possibly be a book of fairy tales), and this is enough to convince him that there must be something in books that, once experienced, makes living life without them meaningless. He realizes that there is a person behind every book. As Nietzsche observed, the system of a philosopher may be dead and debunked, but the *person* behind it is incontrovertible; the person simply cannot be killed. At any rate, books at this early stage of nihilism seem to represent a counter-ideal, offering a kind of transcendence (books themselves are often compared to upwardly soaring birds) of his situation and a new relationship to time (the kind of expansive and dreaming time associated with reverie). Soon following this incident, an intense physical need to read the books he has stolen overcomes him. Now he vomits from the smell of kerosene, and there is a period of convalescence during which the fever works itself out in terms of the search for new values:

> So it was the hand that started it all. He felt one hand and then the other work his coat free and let it slump to the floor. He held his pants out into an abyss and let them fall into darkness. His hands had been infected, and soon it would be his arms. He could feel the poison working up his wrists and into his elbows and his shoulders, and then the jumpover from shoulder blade to shoulder blade like a spark leaping a gap. His hands were ravenous. And his eyes were beginning to feel hunger, as if they must look at something, anything, everything.

In his culture criticism, Nietzsche distinguishes neatly between one kind of cultural health that is defensive and restrictive and another that is marked by an abundant strength and vitality. Fire Chief Beatty is an example of this former idea of cultural health, . . . but in this passage is implicitly the idea that Montag's illness will have a positive value and may even strengthen him. True, it exposes old illusions to an abyss, but it also bridges a gap between Montag and himself. Sickness is, then, actually good for Montag, a desirable challenge stimulating his powers. Montag now wants to see everything outside himself, is ravenously hungry for a world outside the self. Such a sickness, once overcome and incorporated, would leave him in a higher and enhanced state of health. Of course, in a sense, this idea of health collides with the romantic notion of perfect health embodied by Clarisse, for she is somehow untainted, untouched, and untroubled by any "Fall" into sickness. She remains the inviolate utopian ideal of the novel, never burnt by the fireflies of any conflagration, and it seems that Bradbury, by having her die early in the novel, never seriously questions that ideal. Montag, however, has to cope with this disease (or dis-ease, as Bradbury spaces it) on her disappearance.

A True Nihilist

Before Montag can begin to read in earnest, however, Fire Chief Beatty arrives to ask him when he will be well again. He gives Montag what he hopes will be an antidote for his sickness, which consists of a lesson in Firemen history. Ironically, that history itself is an incisive indictment of the American culture industry because it is an example of the many forms of distorted communication that take place in it, from outright censorship of forbidden books (Bradbury sees this as an extension of trends in the 1950s, of course) to ideology and its leveling of all values to the unconscious and barbaric repetition of the same. Like a machine rotating on the same spot, Beatty's rhetoric gives us the impression of life and vitality, but it actually has none. . . .

What Beatty fears most is our present cultural situation with its conflict of interpretations. He only wants people to be crammed full of positivist facts (even though he ridicules the scientific explanation of fire in terms of friction and molecules as "gobbledygook") that do not change, like the fact, worn as an emblem on every fireman's arm, that book paper catches fire and burns at $451°$F. His entire history is negative and defensive because he cannot affirm differences that are a result of the will to power playing itself out in the historical field. Beatty really is, then, at bottom a nihilist because he thinks that the sight of such a bleak and useless existence as man has discovered in this century and the last has made him feel only bestial and lonely. Beatty knows that man has lost dignity in his own eyes to an incredible extent in trying to equate the universe. . . .

Feeding Montag's Hunger

It becomes obvious in the second part of the novel . . . that Montag's hunger cannot be satisfied by the spectacles of the mass media. Indeed, this society seems to have lost the knowledge of the real feeling of satisfaction. It is only when Montag reaches Faber, an old retired English teacher, that he receives something like an antidote to his dis-ease. . . .

Faber introduces Montag to reveries of the earth and the will, but not before telling him that he is a "hopeless roman-

tic" for believing that books themselves are what he needs or
that they themselves are transcendences of life. Faber tells
Montag that books are hated and feared because they show
the pores in the face of life. Furthermore, on close inspection
by the intellect, they reveal themselves precisely as texts,
which "stitch the patches of the universe together into one
garment for us." That is their only magic. In books, which can
always be shown to be texts, the human will to truth cannot
become total. We are allowed the play of interpretation. This
is quite unlike the spectacle of the mass media, where the environment is as real as the world: "It *becomes* and is the truth."
Nonetheless, and in spite of these indications of critical reading Faber wants to inculcate in Montag, he also tries to
awaken in him a nostalgia for the meaning of the earth. In fact
Faber tells him a myth:

> "We are living in a time when flowers are trying to live on
> flowers, instead of growing on good rain and black loam. Even
> fireworks, for all their prettiness, come from the chemistry of
> the earth. Yet somehow we think we can grow, feeding on
> flowers and fireworks, without completing the cycle back to re-
> ality. Do you know the legend of Hercules and Antaeus, the gi-
> ant wrestler, whose strength was incredible so long as he stood
> firmly on earth? But when he was held, rootless, in midair, by
> Hercules, he perished easily. If there isn't something in that
> legend for us today, in this city, in our time, I am completely in-
> sane."

Faber arranges to read to Montag more of this wisdom of
the earth from the book of Job by implanting an electronic device in his ear (a creative use of this medium). Listening to the
delicate filigree of the old man's voice in the following days
and "nights when there was a very bright moon shining on
the earth," Montag's imagination produces its own antidote
through a reverie of the earth. He imagines that fire and water, Montag plus Faber, will combine to form a new substance, a new self, symbolized by wine. . . . Montag needs this
reverie to believe in his own value again. Faber destroys Montag's romantic illusions, but nonetheless rescues him from total nihilism by providing him with a myth to awaken his
dreaming capacity. It awakens in Montag the desire for a kind
of instinctive knowledge of the body, but certainly not a longing for another world. These values are, in turn, revalued at
the end of Part Three.

I mentioned above a series of reveries leading up to this
revaluation and reversal. They come after Montag has burned

his own house in a conflagration that also kills Beatty and destroys a mechanical hound and after he has escaped from the city. The most important one for present purposes is the long water reverie, of which we can only examine a sample here. In it, Montag learns to "will backwards," to affirm the passage of time and to liberate himself from the entire weight of the negative. Floating peacefully on his back in a river, looking at the reflected light of the moon, Montag realizes that all knowledge is "solar," that is, active interpretation. As Nietzsche would say, there is no immaculate perception (See *Thus Spoke Zarathustra*, trans. Kaufmann, Second Part, "On Redemption" for willing backwards, and "On Immaculate Perception"). He cannot, like the Moon, simply reflect in contemplation his love of the Earth. It must be willed:

> The sun burnt every day. It burnt Time. The world rushed in a circle and turned on its axis and time was busy burning the years and the people anyway, without any help from him. So if he burnt things with the firemen and the sun burnt Time, that meant *everything* burnt!
>
> One of them had to stop burning. The sun wouldn't, certainly. So it looked as if it had to be Montag and the people he had worked with until a few short hours ago. . . .

The realization that things go in cycles of nihilism, without the ego consciously willing it, could crush Montag at this point if he were not protected by the water of his reverie. Here again we have the image of nihilism as a fire that inexhaustibly and voraciously appropriates everything strange or new in life with a view to reducing it to sameness. If allowed to progress to the limit, it would reduce all values to falsity (the essence of Beatty's reading of texts). To overcome himself, Montag the fireman vows never to burn again. This is an affirmation, not a negation—one that furthermore affirms everything against which Beatty directed his destructive dialectic. It is the emergence of differences and the will affirming and interpreting itself in time. Montag realizes that the world is full of burning of all types and sizes but also that "the guild of the asbestos weaver must open shop very soon," weaving myths and texts, no doubt, that will sustain humanity. It is only thus that the becoming of the world can be redeemed, and Montag goes on to dream forwards about Clarisse in a vision of the utopian ideal, never burnt by the fireflies of any conflagration. After this reverie in which he interprets his life backwards and forwards in time, he emerges from the river a happy man, discovering delight in the miraculous presence of objects liberated from the oblivion in which technological thinking casts them. . . .

In the novel's last few sentences, Montag is a man who has mastered a great inner chaos and who now feels not emptiness, but a kind of instinctive memory, the "slow stir of words, the slow simmer." He speaks from an initial happiness and plenitude, from a sense of a new beginning that is also linked to tradition (quoting from the Bible), three times reiterating the word "yes." What could be more appropriate, then, that Montag should quote words from the Apocalypse of St. John, the lines about the tree of life, rooted now in *this* world, whose leaves are for the healing of nations?

CHAPTER 3

A Reflection of the Real World

Fahrenheit 451 Is a Reflection of 1950s America

Jack Zipes

Fahrenheit 451 is often discussed in terms of universal issues, such as technological change or modern mass culture, writes Jack Zipes in the following essay. Critics who see the book in such broad terms may fail to realize how precisely it is tied to the reality of the United States in the early 1950s. Zipes examines the novel in light of the U.S. political and intellectual climate at the time it was published, and finds in the novel symbolic representations of specifically American problems. Zipes is coeditor of the *Lion and Unicorn*, a journal for discussion of literature for children.

Perhaps it is endemic to academic criticism of science fiction to talk in abstractions and haggle over definitions of utopia, dystopia, fantasy, science, and technology. Questions of rhetoric, semiotic codes, structure, motifs, and types take precedence over the historical context of the narrative and its sociopolitical implications. If substantive philosophical comments are made, they tend to be universal statements about humanity, art, and the destiny of the world. Such is the case with Ray Bradbury's *Fahrenheit 451*. As a result, we hear that the novel contains a criticism of "too rapid and pervasive technological change" within a tradition of "humanistic conservatism."[1] Or, it is actually "the story of Bradbury, disguised as Montag and his lifelong affair with books" and contains his major themes: "the freedom of the mind, the evocation of the past; the desire for Eden; the integrity of the individual; the allurements and traps of the future."[2] One critic has interpreted the novel as portraying a "conformist hell."[3] Another regards it as a social commentary about the

Abridged from Jack Zipes, "Mass Degradation of Humanity and Massive Contradictions in Bradbury's Vision of America in *Fahrenheit 451*," in *No Place Else: Explorations in Utopian and Dystopian Fiction*, edited by Eric S. Rabkin, Martin H. Greenberg, and Joseph D. Olander. Copyright © 1983 by the Board of Trustees, Southern Illinois University. Reprinted by permission of Southern Illinois University Press.

present which levels a critique at "the emptiness of modern mass culture and its horrifying effects."[4]

All these interpretations are valid because they are so general and apparent, but they could also pertain to anyone or anything that lived in a "little cow town." Their difficulty is that they form abstractions about figures already extrapolated from a particular moment in American history, and these abstractions are not applied to the particular moment as it informs the text, but to the universe at large. Thus, *Fahrenheit 451* is discussed in terms of the world's problems at large when it is essentially bound to the reality of the early 1950s in America, and it is the specificity of the crises endangering the fabric of American society which stamps the narrative concern. The McCarthy witch hunts, the Cold War, the Korean War, the rapid rise of television as a determinant in the culture industry, the spread of advertisement, the abuse of technology within the military-industrial complex, the frustration and violence of the younger generation, the degradation of the masses[5]—these are the factors which went into the making of *Fahrenheit 451* as an American novel, and they form the parameters of any discussion of the dystopian and utopian dimensions of this work.

Bradbury is an eminently careful and conscious writer, and he always has specific occurrences and conditions in mind when he projects into the future. In *Fahrenheit 451*, he was obviously reacting to the political and intellectual climate of his times and intended to play the sci-fi game of the possible with his readers of 1953. This game . . . depends on the author's rhetorical ability to create a mode of discourse which allows him to exaggerate, intensify, and extend scientific, technological, and social conditions from a current real situation to their most extreme point while convincing the reader that everything which occurs in the fantasy world is feasible in the distant future. Belief in reality is at no time expected to be suspended. On the contrary, the reader is expected to bear in mind the reality of his/her situation to be able to draw comparisons and appropriate correspondences with the fictional correlates which are projections not only of the author's imagination but of the probabilities emanating from the social tendencies of the author's environment. Thus, in *Fahrenheit 451* specific American problems of the early 1950s are omnipresent and are constantly projected into the future, estranged, negated, and finally exploded in

the hope that more positive values might be reborn from the
ashes in phoenix-like manner. *Fahrenheit 451* is structured
around fire and death as though it were necessary to con-
ceive new rituals and customs from the ashes of an America
bent on destroying itself and possibly the world. Bradbury's
vision of America and Americans assumes the form of the
sci-fi game of the possible because he wants it to be played
out in reality. That is, the ethical utopian rigor of the book
imbues the metaphorical images with a political gesture
aimed at influencing the reader's conscience and subsequent behavior in society. While Bradbury obviously takes a
position against the mass degradation of humanity, there are
curious massive contradictions in his illumination of social
tendencies which make his own position questionable. Let
us try to recast the discursive mode of the narrative in light
of the sociopolitical context of Bradbury's day to see what he
perceived in the social tendencies of the 1950s and what alternative paths he illuminated in anticipation of possible cat-
astrophes.

THE AMERICAN MALE OF 1950

First, a word about Montag and his situation at the beginning of the novel. As a law-enforcer, Montag symbolizes
those forces of repression which were executing the orders
of McCarthy supporters and the conservative United States
government led by General Dwight D. Eisenhower, John
Foster Dulles, and J. Edgar Hoover. He is not a simple law officer but belongs to the special agency of liquidation and espionage, similar to the FBI and CIA. Moreover, he is an in-
sider, who at thirty years of age has reached full manhood
and is perhaps at his most virile stage. This is exactly why
he was created and chosen by Bradbury. At thirty, as we
know from real life and from numerous other novels of the
twentieth century,[6] Montag is also entering a critical stage
and is most susceptible to outside influences. Therefore, he
is perfect for initiating the game of the possible. Montag likes
his job. He gets pleasure out of burning, and his virility is
closely linked to "the brass nozzle in his fists, with this great
python spitting its venomous kerosene upon the world." We
first encounter Montag in a fit of orgasm, idealistically ful-
filling his mission of purging the world of evil books. The
image of book-burning, the symbolic helmet, the uniform
with a salamander on the arm and a phoenix disc on his

chest suggest a situation of the past, namely the Nazis, swastikas, and book-burning of the 1930s. But it is not far from the realm of possibility in the early 1950s of America that Montag as an American fireman might be pouring kerosene over books and burning them. The censorship of books which dealt with socialism, eroticism, and sexuality in the early 1950s made the extension of Montag's actions conceivable for Bradbury and his readers. Indeed, *Fahrenheit 451* begins with an acceptable statement for the silent 1950s in America which demanded a silence to all dissent: "It was a pleasure to burn." Here male identity is immediately associated with liquidation and destruction, with dictatorial power. Bradbury plays with the unconscious desires of the American male and extends them into the future as reality while at the same time he immediately questions that reality and machoism through Montag's misgivings.

The narrative thread of the American male vision of 1950 hangs on Montag's piecing together what has made him into the man he is at age thirty so that he can pursue a more substantial and gratifying life. This means that he must undo social entanglements, expose his understanding to the world, and burn in a different way than he does at the beginning of the narrative. His sight is our sight. His possibilities are our possibilities. His discourse with the world is ours. What he does in the future corresponds to the tasks set for us in the 1950s which may still be with us now. Though not exactly a *Bildungsroman, Fahrenheit 451* is a novel of development in that Montag undergoes a learning experience which lends the book its utopian impetus. Let us consider the main stages of Montag's learning experiences because they constitute Bradbury's angry critique of America—and here we must remember that Bradbury was writing about the same time as the Angry Young Generation in England and the Beat Generation in America, groups of writers who rejected the affluence and vacuousness of technological innovation in capitalist societies.

AN ANGRY CRITIQUE OF AMERICA

The first phase of Montag's learning experience is initiated by Clarisse McClellan, who makes him wonder why people talk and why he does not pay attention to small things. The name Clarisse suggests light, clarity, and illumination, and Montag must be enlightened. His own ability to discuss, see, feel, and hear has been muted. He is unconscious of his own history and the forces acting on him. Clarisse infers that his consciousness has been stunted by the two-hundred-foot-long billboards, the parlour walls, races, and fun parks, all of which she avoids because they prevent her from being alone with her own thoughts. Thus, she illuminates the way Montag must take not only for his own self-questioning but for the reader's own questioning of the consciousness industry in America. Bradbury wants to get at the roots of American conformity and immediately points a finger at the complicity of state and industry for using technology to produce television programs, gambling sports games, amusement parks, and advertising to block self-reflection and blank out the potential for alternative ways of living which do not conform to fixed national standards. As Bradbury's mouthpiece, Clarisse wonders whether Montag is actually happy leading a death-in-life, and Montag quickly realizes that he is not happy when he enters his sterile and fully automatic house. He proceeds to the room where his wife Mildred is ostensibly sleeping and senses that "the room was cold but nonetheless he felt he could not breathe. He did not wish to open the curtains and open the french windows, for he did not want the moon to come into the room. So, with the feeling of a man who will die in the next hour for lack of air, he felt his way toward his open, separate, and therefore cold bed." The image of death is fully impressed upon him when he becomes aware that his wife has attempted suicide. This is startling, but what is even more startling for Montag is the mechanical, indifferent way the operators treat his wife with a machine that revives her by pumping new blood into her system. Moreover, he becomes highly disturbed when the pill given to his wife by the operators makes her unaware the next morning that she had tried to take her own life. Montag witnesses—because Clarisse has made him more sensitive—the manner in which technology is being used even in the field of medicine to deaden the senses while keeping people alive as machines. He is part of the deadening process. In fact, dead himself he now begins to rise from the ashes like the phoenix. He is testing wings which he never thought he had.

Clarisse is his first teacher, the one who teaches him how to fly. For one intensive week he meets with Clarisse, who instructs him through her own insight and experience why and how the alleged antisocial and disturbed people may have a higher regard for society and be more sane than those who declare themselves normal and uphold the American way of life. Bradbury attacks the American educational system through Clarisse's description of classes in school which are centered on mass media and sports and prevent critical discussion. Schooling is meant to exhaust the young so that they are tame, but the frustration felt by the young is then expressed in their "fun" outside the school, which always turns to violence. Communication gives way to games of beating up people, destroying things, and playing games like chicken. Clarisse admits that she is "'afraid of children my own age. They kill each other. Did it always used to be that way? My uncle says no. Six of my friends have been shot in the last year alone. Ten of them died in car wrecks. I'm afraid of them and they don't like me because I'm afraid.'" But it is not simply fear that cannot be shown in public but all kinds of feelings. Form has subsumed emotions and substance, dissipated humanity, so that the medium has become the message. Art has become abstract, and people are identified with the things they own. They themselves are to be purchased, used, and disposed of in an automatic way.

Montag's life was in the process of becoming a permanent fixture in a system of degradation, but it was fortunately upset by Clarisse for a week. And she upsets it again by disappearing. Despite her disappearance, she has already served an important purpose because Montag is now somewhat more capable of learning from his own experiences, and he moves into his second phase. Significantly it begins with his entering the firehouse where he will start doubting his profession. The mood is set by the firemen playing cards in the tidy, polished firehouse, idling away the time until they can destroy, and the "radio hummed somewhere ... war may be declared any hour. This country stands ready to defend its—." Throughout the novel, war lurks in the background until it finally erupts. The obvious reference here is to the Cold War and the Korean War which might lead to such an atomic explosion as that which occurs at the end of the book. Again the media spread one-sided news about the nation's cause, driving the people hysterically to war instead of convincing them to seek means for communication and co-existence.

BLAMING THE PEOPLE

Montag gradually learns how the government manipulates the masses through the media, shows of force, and legal measures to pursue its own ends. His first lesson is quick and simple when he discusses a man who was obviously sane but was taken to an insane asylum because he had been reading books and had built his own library. Captain Beatty remarks: "'Any man's insane who thinks he can fool the Government and us.'" Montag's next lesson comes from his direct experience of witnessing a woman destroy herself because her books are burned by the firemen. This incident causes Montag to bring a book back to his own house and to question what it is in books that would make a woman want to stay in a burning house. For the first time in his life he realizes that human effort and feelings go into the making of a book, and he resolves, despite a warning visit from Beatty, to pursue an experiment with his wife so that they can understand why their lives are in such a mess. Beatty had already attempted to give a false historical explanation of how firemen had been organized by Benjamin Franklin to burn English-influenced books. This time he tries a different ploy by placing the responsibility on the people and arguing that the different ethnic minority and interest groups did not want controversial subjects aired in books. This led to vapid and insipid publications. "'But the public, knowing what it wanted, spinning happily, let the comic-books survive. And the three-dimensional sex-magazines, of course. There you have it, Montag. It didn't come from the Government down. There was no dictum, no declaration, no censorship, to start with, no! Technology, mass exploitation, and minority pressure carried the trick, thank God. Today, thanks to them, you can stay happy all the time, you are allowed to read comics, the good old confessions, or trade-journals.'"

Thus, in Beatty's view—one which, incidentally is never contradicted by Bradbury—the firemen are keepers of peace. He cynically argues that the profession of firemen had to expand to keep the people happy and satisfy their complaints. This is why it conducts espionage and has a computerized system to keep track of each and every citizen in the United States. Yet, despite Beatty's explanation, Montag is firm in his resolution, for he suspects that there is more to Beatty's analysis than meets the eye. Intuitively he recalls Clarisse's discussion about her uncle and the front porches which were eliminated from people's homes because the architects (i.e., the government) did not want people to be active, talking, and communicating with one another. This is why it has become so important for him to talk to his wife and share the experiment in reading with her. However, she has been too conditioned by the television parlour games and by the seashell in her ear—the electronic waves which broadcast music and programs to prevent her thinking. Therefore, Montag is now forced to seek help from Faber, a retired English professor, who had been dismissed from the last liberal arts college because the humanities had in effect been dismissed from the educational system.

COMMANDING HIS OWN DESTINY

By establishing contact with Faber, whose name connotes maker or builder, Montag enters into his third stage of learning experience and begins to assume command of his own destiny. Faber teaches him that the alienation and conformity in society have not been caused by machines but by human beings who have stopped reading of their own accord, and that too few resisted the trend toward standardization and degradation of humanity—including himself. However, Montag gives him hope and courage. So he decides to begin subversive activities with a printer and to set up a communication system with Montag which will depend on the fireman's initiative. He gives Montag a green bullet through which they can communicate and plan their activities without being observed. Here technology is employed to further emancipatory and humanistic interests. The green bullet will also allow Faber to share his knowledge with Montag so that the latter will begin to think for himself. After a violent outburst at home which he knows will end his relationship with Mildred for good, Montag knows that he has made a complete rupture with his former life and recognizes the significance of his relationship with Faber. "On the way downtown he was so completely alone with his terrible error that he felt the necessity for the strange warmness and goodness that came from a familiar and gentle voice speaking in the night. Already, in a few short hours, it seemed that he had known Faber a lifetime. Now he knew that he was two people, that he was above all Montag, who knew nothing, who did not even know himself a fool, but only suspected it. And he knew also that he was the old man who talked to him and talked to him as the train was sucked from one end of the night city to the other one on a long sickening gasp of motion." From this point on Montag moves toward regaining touch with his innermost needs and desires, and he will not be sucked into anything. He avoids the trap set for him by Beatty and burns his real enemies for the first time. His flight from the claws of the mechanical hound, which represents all the imaginative technological skills of American society transformed into a ruthless monster and used to obliterate dissenting humanity, is like the flight of the phoenix born again. Not only is Montag a new person, but he also invigorates Faber, who feels alive for the first time in years. It is a period of war on all fronts, a period of destruction and negation which is reflective of the Cold War, the Korean War, and the oppressive political climate of the 1950s. Yet, there are signs that a new, more humane world might develop after the turmoil ends.

Montag's last phase of learning is a spiritual coming into his own. He escapes to the outside world and follows the abandoned railroad track which leads him to a man whose name, Granger, indicates that he is a shepherd. Granger takes him to the collective of rebels, who are largely intellectuals. Here Bradbury suggests—as he does in many of his works—that the anti-intellectual strain in America forces most intellectuals to take an outsider position from which it is difficult to influence people. The tendency in America is to drive forward without a humanistic intellectual core.[7] Still, Montag learns that certain intellectuals have not abandoned the struggle to assert themselves and still want to assume a responsible role *within* society. Granger informs him:

> "All we want to do is keep the knowledge we think we will need, intact and safe. We're not out to incite or anger anyone yet. For if we are destroyed, the knowledge is dead, perhaps for good. We are model citizens, in our own special way; we walk the old tracks, we lie in the hills at night, and the city people let us be. We're stopped and searched occasionally, but there's nothing on our persons to incriminate us. The organization is flexible, very loose, and fragmentary. Some of us have had plastic surgery on our faces and fingerprints. Right now we have a horrible job; we're waiting for the war to begin and, as quickly, end. It's not pleasant, but then we're not in control, we're the odd minority crying in the wilderness. When the war's over, perhaps we can be of some use in the world."

By the end of his adventures, there is very little that Montag can learn from his mentors anymore. That is, he will undoubtedly continue to share their knowledge, but he, too, has become an imparter of knowledge. He takes the world into himself and becomes at one with it. The notions of the Book of Ecclesiastes are carried by him, and he will spread its humanistic message to help heal the rifts in the world. There is a suggestion at the end of the novel that the American society is largely responsible for the wars and destruction brought upon itself. A time has come, a season, Montag envisions, for building up. He is no longer a fireman but a prophet of humanity. The dystopian critique gives way to a utopian vision.

NOTES

1. A. James Stupple, "The Past, the Future, and Ray Bradbury," in *Voices for the Future*, ed. Thomas D. Clareson (Bowling Green: Bowling Green Univ. Popular Pr., 1976), p. 24.

2. Willis E. NcNelly, "Ray Bradbury—Past, Present, and Future," in *Voices for the Future*, pp. 169, 173.

3. Kingsley Amis, *New Maps of Hell* (New York: Harcourt, Brace, 1960), p. 110.

4. Joseph Blakey, *Fahrenheit 451* (Toronto: 1972), Coles Notes, pp. 90–91.

5. For good background material on this period, see Daniel Snowman, *America Since 1920* (New York: Harper and Row, 1968); I.F. Stone, *The Haunted Fifties* (London: Merlin, 1964); and Howard Zinn, *Postwar America* (Indianapolis: Bobbs-Merrill, 1973).

6. See Theodore Ziolkowski, *Fictional Transfigurations of Jesus* (Princeton: Princeton Univ. Pr., 1972). Like Jesus Christ, who went out preaching at age thirty, Montag has features of a Christ figure.

7. See Richard Hofstadter, *Anti-intellectualism in American Life* (New York: Knopf, 1963).

Bradbury's Cold War Novels: *Fahrenheit 451* and *The Martian Chronicles*

Kevin Hoskinson

Bradbury was not predicting the future in his two cold war novels, reports Kevin Hoskinson. He was, instead, attempting to *prevent* the world from heading in the direction it seemed to be going. Although *The Martian Chronicles* and *Fahrenheit 451* are very different books, both examine such central issues as how the advent of the atomic age suddenly made human existence seem very precarious. Hoskinson is an associate professor of developmental English at Lorain County Community College in Elyria, Ohio.

In a discussion about the thematic content of *The Martian Chronicles* with interviewer David Mogen in 1980, Ray Bradbury stated, "*The Martian Chronicles* and *Fahrenheit 451* come from the same period in my life, when I was warning people. I was *preventing* futures." In this pairing of the two books, Bradbury suggests a deep kinship between the pieces and indicates the probability that they are more than just successive novels in his overall body of work.[1] Though the two fictions are usually read as separate entities, if read as complementary works, they provide a more comprehensive view of a larger whole. As consecutive arrivals in Bradbury's postwar publications, and in their mutual attraction to similar major themes of the cold war era, *The Martian Chronicles* and *Fahrenheit 451* distinguish themselves as Bradbury's "cold war novels."

The two works are on the surface entirely different kinds of fiction. *The Martian Chronicles* is a collection of twenty-

Excerpted from Kevin Hoskinson, "*The Martian Chronicles* and *Fahrenheit 451:* Ray Bradbury's Cold War Novels," *Extrapolation*, vol. 36, no. 4 (Winter 1995), pp. 345–59. Reprinted by permission of The Kent State University Press. (References cited in the original have been omitted from this reprint.)

six chapters (most originally published as short stories), written between 1944 and 1950 and linked primarily by their setting on the planet Mars between the years 1999 and 2026. Since many of the stories were separately conceived, most of the characters in the finished book are contained within their initial tales and do not cross over into other chapters. And though Mars itself is in many ways the centerpiece of the book, and its treatment by the humans is "chronicled" over a twenty-seven-year period, there is no "protagonist" in the pure sense of the term, nor is there a "plot" common to the separate sections. In contrast, *Fahrenheit 451* is structured as a novel, divided into three chapters; it is set on Earth; it is the story of one central protagonist, Guy Montag; and the plot of the novel—Montag's liberation from Captain Beatty and his acceptance of a new purpose in a new civilization—is carefully mapped out.

These surface differences of structure, character, and setting notwithstanding, *The Martian Chronicles* and *Fahrenheit 451* share a distinction as "cold war fiction" because in them, much more deliberately than in earlier or later publications, Bradbury deals with subjects and issues that were shaped by the political climate of the United States in the decade immediately following World War II.[2] A number of significant events during these years transformed the character of America from a supremely confident, Nazi-demolishing world leader to a country with deep insecurities, one suddenly suspicious and vigilant of Communist activity within its citizenry. First, Joseph Stalin's immediate and unchecked occupation of Eastern European countries at the close of World War II left many Americans wondering if the United States and the Roosevelt administration hadn't foolishly misjudged Soviet intentions at the Yalta Conference in 1945. Second, the Soviet Union's subsequent acquisition of atomic weapons technology by 1949 would reinforce this position; it would also end the U.S. monopoly on thermonuclear weapons and raise questions about Communist agents in high-level government positions. Third, Senator Joseph McCarthy's public accusations of Communist activity in the State Department in 1950 (together with the inflammatory tactics of J. Edgar Hoover, the FBI, and a host of other right-wing government agencies) planted seeds of paranoia and subversion in the American culture that would blossom into fear and irrationality throughout the 1950s. As

David Halberstam points out, "It was a mean time. The nation was ready for witch-hunts" (9). Through his examination of government oppression of the individual, the hazards of an atomic age, recivilization of society, and the divided nature of the "Cold War Man," Ray Bradbury uses *The Martian Chronicles* and *Fahrenheit 451* to expose the "meanness" of the cold war years.

A MEAN TIME

During the Truman years of the early cold war, when the administration attempted to reverse the image of the Democratic party as being "soft" on communism, the U.S. government attempted to silence individuals who were thought to be "potentially disloyal" through various offices such as the Justice Department and the Loyalty Review Board. Truman himself released a press statement in July 1950 that granted authority over national security matters to the FBI. The statement expressed grave concern over "the Godless Communist Cause" and further warned that "it is important to learn to know the enemies of the American way of life" (Theoharis 141–42). For Bradbury, such government-supported conformism amounted to censorship and ultimately led to the fostering of what William F. Touponce labels "mass culture" (46) and what Kingsley Amis calls "conformist hell" (110). We see Bradbury's strong distrust of "majority-held" views and official doctrine positions in several places in *The Martian Chronicles;* these areas of distrust, moreover, recur in *Fahrenheit 451.*

In the seventh chapter of *Chronicles,* "—And the Moon Be Still as Bright" (originally published in 1948), the fierceness of the individual and the official will of the majority clash violently in the persons of Jeff Spender and Captain Wilder. . . .

Bradbury picks up this theme of distrust for the officially endorsed view again in "Usher II," the seventeenth chapter of *Chronicles* (originally published in 1950 prior to the publication of the full book). In this chapter William Stendahl designs a replica of Edgar Allan Poe's House of Usher on Mars. His intent is twofold: to pay tribute to Poe and "to teach [the Clean-Minded people] a fine lesson for what [they] did to Mr. Poe on Earth," which was to burn his works (along with the works of others who wrote "tales of the future") in the Great Fire of 1975. Here again Bradbury rejects the will of the majority through Stendahl's speech to Bigelow, the architect of Usher II. Stendahl sermonizes to Bigelow that the Great Fire came about because "there was always a minority afraid of something, and a great majority afraid of the dark, afraid of the future, afraid of the past, afraid of the present, afraid of themselves and shadows of themselves." Another neurosis Bradbury places in Stendahl's litany of fears has roots in the "red scare" policies enacted through McCarthyist tactics in 1950s America: "Afraid of the word 'politics' (which eventually became a synonym for Communism among the more reactionary elements, so I hear, and it was worth your life to use the word!). . ."[3] Later, at the party Stendahl throws for his invited guests, the Moral Climates people, Stendahl kills all the "majority guests" with different approaches to murders seen in Poe's stories.[4] At the end of the chapter, Stendahl mortars up Moral Climates Investigator Garrett into a brick wall because Garrett "took other people's advice that [Poe's books] needed burning." In contrast with "—And the Moon Be Still as Bright," where the individual is martyred by the majority, the individual in "Usher II" enjoys a sinister triumph over the majority.

AN ATTACK ON CENSORSHIP

In *Fahrenheit 451* Bradbury resumes his attack on government-based censorship encountered earlier in "Usher II." Set on Earth rather than on Mars, this novel follows the metamorphosis of Guy Montag, a fireman (a starter of fires in this future dystopian society) who comes to question and break free of the government that employs him to burn books. The novel opens with Montag having just returned to the firehouse after igniting another residence, "grinn[ing] the fierce grin of all men singed and driven back by flame". He is clearly of the majority at this point, loyal to his job and proud of wearing the salamander and the phoenix disc, the official insignia of the Firemen of America. But seventeen-year-old Clarisse McClellan, who is dangerous in Beatty's eyes because "she [doesn't] want to know *how* a thing [is] done, but *why*," points out some disturbing facts that Montag cannot escape: he answers her questions quickly without thinking; he can't remember if he knew there was dew on early-morning grass or not; he can't answer the question of whether he is happy or not. A growing unrest with his own lack of individual sensibilities creeps into Montag at Clarisse's challenges. As Donald Watt observes, Clarisse is "catalytic" and "dominant in Montag's growth to awareness" (197); her role for Montag parallels the role of Spender for Captain Wilder, planting the seed of doubt that enacts a process of critical self-examination. These doubts about the government he is serving accumulate through the latest suicide attempt by Montag's wife, Mildred (and her casual acceptance of this attempt after she is resuscitated); through his witnessing of a book-hoarding woman who chose to ignite her own home rather than flee in the face of the firemen's flamethrowers; through the government's systematic elimination of Clarisse; through his own growing need to read and understand books.

Montag ultimately realizes that he cannot return to the firehouse. At this point he rejects both the realm of the majority and his association with Chief Beatty, who professes to "stand against the small tide of those who want to make everyone unhappy with conflicting theory and thought." Montag's liberation from the Firemen of America is augmented when he locates Faber (a former English professor and current member of the book-preserving underground), who offers Montag moral counsel and employs him as an infiltrator at the firehouse. Mildred, in the meantime, breaks her silence and sounds a fire alarm at the Montag residence. In a dramatic confrontation of Individual vs. State, Montag . . . turns the flamethrower on Beatty. This revolt severs Montag from the majority permanently; he then joins the underground movement to preserve books for the future as global war descends on the city.

THE ATOMIC AGE

Another theme of the cold war years Bradbury takes up in both novels is the precariousness of human existence in an atomic age. The eventual "success" of the Manhattan Project in 1945, which resulted in the development of the atomic bomb, came about only after several years' worth of blind groping toward the right physics equations by some of the brightest physicists in the world.[5] The scientists were literally guessing about how to detonate the bomb, how big to make the bomb, and, most significantly, how strong the bomb would be. The project itself, in the words of Lansing Lamont, was "a bit like trying to manufacture a new automobile with no opportunity to test the engine beforehand" (50). After studying various reports on a wide range of explosions in known history, the Los Alamos physicists determined that the atom bomb's force would fall somewhere in between the volcanic eruption of Krakatau in 1883 (which killed 36,000 people and was heard 3,000 miles away) and the 1917 explosion of the munitions ship *Mont Blanc* in Halifax Harbor, Nova Scotia (killing 1,100)—"hopefully a lot closer to Halifax" Lamont notes, but just where [the scientists] couldn't be sure" (51-52). The subsequent explosions at Hiroshima and Nagasaki made Americans more "sure" of the bomb's potential but not sure at all about whether the knowledge of its potential was worth the price of having created it in the first place. As a line of military defense against the spread of nazism, the bomb became a prime example of how science unleashed can, according to Gary Wolfe, produce "the alienation of humanity from the very technological environments it has constructed in order to resolve its alienation from the universe" (128).

It is difficult to comprehend the depth to which the atom bomb terrified the world, and America specifically, in the early cold war era. Richard Rhodes, author of the *The Making of the Atomic Bomb*, writes that "A nuclear weapon is in fact a total-death machine, compact and efficient" (746) and quotes a Japanese study that concludes that the explosions at Hiroshima and Nagasaki were "the opening chapter to the annihilation of mankind." More than any single technological development, the atomic bomb made people think seriously about the end of the world. As a passport to Wolfe's icon of the wasteland, the bomb "teaches us that the unknown always remains, ready to reassert itself, to send us back to the beginning" (147).

Bradbury first captures the general sense of anxiety felt in a new atomic age in the fifth chapter of *The Martian Chronicles*, "The Taxpayer." This short chapter identifies fear of nuclear war as an impetus for leaving Earth; the chapter also establishes itself as one of several in *Chronicles* that serve as precursors to *Fahrenheit 451* and centralize many of the early cold war themes Bradbury resumes in the second book: "There was going to be a big atomic war on Earth in about two years, and he didn't want to be here when it happened. He and thousands of others like him, if they had any sense, would go to Mars. See if they wouldn't! To get away from wars and censorship and statism and conscription and government control of this and that, of art and science!". . .

Fahrenheit 451 resumes the examination of precarious existence in an atomic age that Bradbury began in *The Martian Chronicles*. Fire as the omnipotent weapon in *Fahrenheit* finds metaphoric parallels in the notion of the bomb as the omnipotent force in the cold war years. The early tests of the Los Alamos project, for example, paid close attention to the extreme temperatures produced by the fissioning and fusioning of critical elements. J. Robert Oppenheimer, Niels Bohr, and Edward Teller based key decisions in the atomic bomb (and later the hydrogen bomb) designs on the core temperatures created at the moment of detonation.[6] Montag and the Firemen of America, likewise, are ever conscious of the key numeral 451 (the temperature at which books burn), so much so that it is printed on their helmets. The linking of hubris with the attainment of power is evident in both the Los Alamos scientists and the Firemen as well. As the Manhattan Project was drawing to a close, the team of physicists who designed the bomb came to exude a high degree of pride in their mastery of science, but without an attendant sense of responsibility. As Lamont explains, the bomb "represented the climax of an intriguing intellectual match between the scientists and the cosmos. The prospect of solving the bomb's cosmic mysteries, of having their calculations proved correct, seemed far more fascinating and important to the scientists than the prospect of their opening an era obsessed by fear and devoted to the control of those very mysteries" (144). *Fahrenheit 451* opens with Montag similarly blinded by his own perceived importance: "He knew that when he returned to the firehouse, he might wink at himself, a minstrel man, burnt-corked, in the mirror. Later, going to sleep, he would feel the fiery smile still gripped by his face muscles, in the dark. It never went away, that smile, it never ever went away, as long as he remembered." Like the engineers of atomic destruction, the engineer of intellectual destruction feels the successful completion of his goals entitles him to a legitimate smugness. The work of the cold war physicists, in retrospect, also shares something else with Montag, which Donald Watt points out: "Montag's destructive burning . . . is blackening, not enlightening; and it poses a threat to nature" (198).

Fahrenheit 451 also expands on the anxiety over the atomic bomb and fear of a nuclear apocalypse introduced in *Chronicles*. In *Fahrenheit*, Beatty endorses the official government position that, as "custodians of our peace of mind," he and Montag should "let [man] forget there is such a thing as war." Once Montag has decided to turn his back on the firehouse, however, he tries conveying his personal sense of outrage to Mildred at being kept ignorant, hoping to incite a similar concern in her: "How in hell did those bombers get up there every single second of our lives! Why doesn't some-one want to talk about it! We've started and won two atomic wars since 1990!" Mildred, however, is perfectly uninspired and breaks off the conversation to wait for the White Clown to enter the TV screen. But Montag's unheeded warning be-comes reality; the bombs are dropped once Montag meets up with Granger and the book people . . . and Montag's hor-rific vision of the bomb's shock wave hitting the building where he imagines Mildred is staying captures a chilling im-age of his ignorant wife's last instant of life:

> Montag, falling flat, going down, saw or felt, or imagined he saw or felt the walls go dark in Millie's face, heard her screaming, because in the millionth part of time left, she saw her own face reflected there, in a mirror instead of a crystal ball, and it was such a wild empty face, all by itself in the room, touching nothing, starved and eating of itself, that at last she recognized it as her own and looked quickly up at the ceiling as it and the entire structure of the hotel blasted down upon her, carrying her with a million pounds of brick, metal, plaster, and wood, to meet other people in the hives below, all on their quick way down to the cellar where the explosion rid itself of them in its own unreasonable way.

Perhaps Bradbury's own sense of fear at a future that must accommodate atomic weapons had intensified between *The Martian Chronicles*'s publication in 1950 and *Fahrenheit 451*'s completion in 1953; perhaps what David Mogen iden-tifies as Bradbury's inspiration for the book, Hitler's book burnings, affords little room for the comic (107). For what-ever reasons, unlike *Chronicles*, which intersperses the solemnity of its nuclear aftermath chapters with a bit of lightness in the Walter Gripp story, *Fahrenheit* sustains a serious tone to the end of the book, even in its resurrection-ist optimism for the future of the arts.

OPTIMISM

This optimism for the future—this notion of recivilization—is the third common element between *The Martian Chroni-cles* and *Fahrenheit 451* that has early cold war connections.

Given such nihilistic phenomena of the cold war era as its tendencies toward censorship, its socially paranoid outlook, and its budding arms race, it may seem a strange period to give rise to any optimism. However, one of the great ironies of the period was a peripheral belief that somehow the presence of nuclear arms would, by their very capacity to bring about ultimate destruction to *all* humans, engender a very special sort of cautiousness and cooperative spirit in the world heretofore not experienced. Perhaps there was a belief that Hiroshima and Nagasaki had taught us a big enough lesson in themselves about nuclear cataclysm that we as humans would rise above our destructive tendencies and live more harmoniously. One very prominent figure who espoused this position was Dr. J. Robert Oppenheimer, the very man who headed the Los Alamos Manhattan Project. Oppenheimer would emerge as one of the most morally intriguing characters of the cold war. He was among the first in the scientific community to encourage restraint, caution, and careful deliberation in all matters regarding the pursuit of atomic energy. "There is only one future of atomic explosives that I can regard with any enthusiasm: that they should never be used in war," he said in a 1946 address before the George Westinghouse Centennial Forum (5). He also refused to participate in the development of the hydrogen bomb following Los Alamos, calling such a weapon "the plague of Thebes" (Rhodes 777).[7] In one of his most inspired addresses on the cooperation of art and science, Oppenheimer stated that "Both the man of science and the man of art live always at the edge of mystery, surrounded by it; both always, as the measure of their creation, have had to do with the harmonization of what is new with what is familiar, with the balance between novelty and synthesis, with the struggle to make partial order in total chaos. They can, in their work and in their lives, help themselves, help one another, and help all men" (145). . . .

Bradbury's optimism for a recivilized world is evident in the conclusion of *Fahrenheit 451*. The seed for an optimistic ending to this dystopian work is actually planted just before the bombs strike. As Montag makes his way across the wilderness, dodging the pursuit of the mechanical hound and the helicopters, he spots the campfire of the book people. His thoughts reflect an epiphany of his transformation from a destroyer of civilization to a builder of it: "[The fire] was not burning. It was *warming.* He saw many hands held to its warmth, hands without arms, hidden in darkness. Above the hands, motionless faces that were only moved and tossed and flickered with firelight. He hadn't known fire could look this way. He had never thought in his life that it could give as well as take." This spirit of giving, of creating from the environment, is emphasized throughout the speeches given by Granger, the leader of the book pre-servers. In his allusion to the phoenix, which resurrects it-self from the ashes of its own pyre, Granger's words reflect the new Montag, who can now see the life-sustaining prop-erties of fire as well as its destructive powers; hopefully, Granger's words also contain hope for the American re-sponse to Hiroshima and Nagasaki: "we've got one damn thing the phoenix never had. We know the damn silly thing we just did. We know all the damn silly things we've done for a thousand years and as long as we know that and always have it around where we can see it, someday we'll stop mak-ing the goddamn funeral pyres and jumping in the middle of them." The book ends with Montag rehearsing in his mind a passage from the Book of Revelation, which he says he'll save for the reading at noon. Peter Sisario sees in this ending "a key to Bradbury's hope that 'the healing of nations' can best come about through a rebirth of man's intellect" (205); Sisario's interpretation of *Fahrenheit*'s ending and Oppen-heimer's interpretation of mankind's necessary response to the cold war share a belief in the triumph of the benevolent side of humans.

COLD WAR MAN

A fourth theme in Bradbury's cold war novels that has a his-torical "objective correlative" is the dichotomous nature of the Cold War Man. The Cold War Man is a man antagonized by conflicting allegiances—one to his government, the other to his personal sense of morals and values—who is forced by circumstance to make an ultimate choice between these impulses. This Bradbury character type has roots in cold war political tensions.

During the early cold war years, the United States's inter-national stance frequently wavered between a policy of mil-itary supremacy and one of peacetime concessions. One his-torian notes this phenomenon in the about-face many Americans took toward Theodore Roosevelt's role in the shifting of global powers following World War II: " . . . both policy and attitude changed with the Truman administration. The rationale behind Yalta—that a negotiated agreement with the Soviet Union was possible and that the development of mutual trust was the best means to a just and lasting peace—was now rejected in favor of the containment policy and superior military strength" (Theoharis 70).

These contradictory stances of peace and aggression in our nation's outlook occasionally found expression in the form of a single man during the early cold war. The figure of Dr. J. Robert Oppenheimer again becomes relevant. Though primarily remembered for his contribution to physics, Oppenheimer also had strong leanings toward the humanities; as a youth and in his years as a Harvard undergraduate, he developed a range of literary interests from the Greek classicists to Donne to Omar Khayyam (Lamont 19). David Halberstam observes, "To some he seemed the divided man— part creator of the most dangerous weapon in history—part the romantic innocent searching for some inner spiritual truth" (33). For a government-employed physicist, however, this "division" would turn out to be something of a tragic flaw in the cold war years. When Oppenheimer would have no part of the U.S. government's decision to pursue the hydrogen bomb in its initial phase of the arms race with the Soviets, the government began an inquiry into his past. It was "determined" in June of 1954 that Oppenheimer was guilty of Communist associations that jeopardized national security.[8] He was then stripped of his government security clearance, and his service with the Atomic Energy Commission terminated. Thus, in Oppenheimer was a man whose pacifistic sympathies eventually triumphed over his capacity for aggression—and in the early cold war years he was punished for it. . . .

The dichotomous Cold War Man theme is treated in *Fahrenheit 451*. Both Montag and Beatty are simultaneously capable of the destructive and appreciative of the artistic. As Donald Watt remarks of Montag, "Burning as constructive energy, and burning as apocalyptic catastrophe, are the symbolic poles of Bradbury's novel" (196). Montag's divided self is clearly displayed by Bradbury at moments when his character is being influenced by the intellectually stimulating presences of Clarisse and Faber. Early in the book, when Montag is just beginning to wrestle with his identity as a fireman, Clarisse tells him that being a fireman "just doesn't seem right for you, somehow." Immediately Bradbury tells us that Montag "felt his body divide itself into a hotness and a coldness, a softness and a hardness, a trembling and a not trembling, the two halves grinding one upon the other." Later, after offering his services to Faber and his group, Montag considers the shiftings of his own character that he has been feeling in his conflicting allegiances: "Now he knew that he was two people, that he was, above all, Montag, who knew nothing, who did not even know himself a fool, but only suspected it. And he knew that he was also the old man who talked to him and talked to him as the train was sucked from one end of the night city to the other." Fire Chief Beatty also suggests aspects of the Cold War Man. In spite of his wearing the role of the Official State Majority Leader as the fire chief and relentlessly burning every book at every alarm, Beatty acknowledges that he knows the history of Nicholas Ridley, the man burned at the stake alluded to by the woman who ignites her own home. He gives Montag the reply that most fire captains are "full of bits and pieces"; however, when he later warns Montag against succumbing to the "itch" to read that every fireman gets "at least once in his career," he further adds an ambiguous disclosure: "Oh, to *scratch* that itch, eh? Well, Montag, take my word for it, I've had to read a few in my time to know what I was about, and the books say *nothing!* Nothing you can teach or believe." Though Beatty has an alibi for having some knowledge of literature, Bradbury urges us to question just what Beatty may *not* be telling us. Montag's later certainty over Beatty's desire to die at Montag's hands raises even more questions about Beatty's commitment to the destructive half of his duality.

Through *The Martian Chronicles* and *Fahrenheit 451*, Ray Bradbury has created a microcosm of early cold war tensions. Though the reader will perceive a degree of Bradbury's sociopolitical concerns from a reading of either novel, it is only through the reading of both as companion pieces that his full cold war vision emerges. From the perspective that America has wrestled itself free of the extremism of the McCarthyists and, thus far, has escaped nuclear war as well, Bradbury's cold war novels may have indeed contributed to the "prevention" of futures with cold war trappings.

NOTES

1. There is a lack of decisiveness among Bradbury scholars as to whether *The Martian Chronicles* is a novel or a collection of short stories with an epicenter of a common world. Much attention has been paid to Bradbury's 1949 encounter with Doubleday Publishing, during which an editor asked Bradbury to piece together his Mars stories and see what happened; no consensus has been reached as to whether the resulting book is a novel or short stories. Mogen describes it both ways, ultimately classifying it in his selected bibliography section of Bradbury's primary sources as a "novel"; Johnson argues for a collection of short stories "adapted and linked together by bridge passages." Bradbury himself has compared the work to Sherwood Anderson's *Winesburg, Ohio,* but he has also called it a novel in other places, suggesting that the distinction is significant only to critics. I prefer the "novel" classification because it seems a more fitting descriptor for a fictional history of Mars than does "short story collection." For a fuller examination of the issue, see Mogen, *Ray Bradbury* 82–93; Johnson, *Ray Bradbury;* and Gallagher, "The Thematic Structure of *The Martian Chronicles.*"

2. It has been asserted in many places among Bradbury scholarship that the Mars created in *The Martian Chronicles* is in one way or another a metaphor for twentieth-century America. Two of the more clearly articulated views on this belong to McNelly and Pell.

3. For two enlightening discussions of the subversive tactics employed by many 1950s right-wing government organizations, see Halberstam and Theoharis.

4. This organization is strongly suggestive of the House Committee on Un-American Activities, a group Halberstam maintains "included a large number of the most unattractive men in American public life—bigots, racists, reactionaries, and sheer buffoons" (12).

5. These minds were, ironically, "true science fictionists" in the Bradbury sense. Bradbury said in 1976 that "science fiction deals with any 'idea' which is not yet born, which wants to come to birth." The atomic bomb became an idea wanting birth in 1939 when Hungarian physicist Leo Szilard solicited Albert Einstein's help in drafting a letter to President Roosevelt, advising the president that, since

Hitler's Germany had successfully produced atomic fission (under Otto Hahn and Fritz Strassman), it would be wise to establish the necessary research to develop a nuclear defense weapon. Los Alamos was conceived of at that point, and science fiction moved closer to science fact. See Jacobs 19 and Lamont 23–25.

6. In fact, the design of the hydrogen bomb was slowed by William Teller's inaccurate calculations regarding the temperature produced when igniting deuterium. The inaccuracy involved the difference between 40 million and 400 million degrees fahrenheit. See Rhodes 418–20.

7. The explosion of one hydrogen bomb is the equivalent of 500 atomic bombs. See Rhodes 418.

8. The actual conviction was one of "'susceptibility' to influences that could endanger the nation's security." Such vagueness pervades the course of the hearings with Oppenheimer. See Lamont 258–91 and Halberstam 342–54.

WORKS CITED

Amis, Kingsley. *New Maps of Hell.* London: Lowe and Brydone, 1960.

Bradbury, Ray. *Fahrenheit 451.* New York: Ballantine, 1953.

———. *The Martian Chronicles.* Garden City, NY: Doubleday, 1950.

Gallagher, Edward J. "The Thematic Structure of *The Martian Chronicles.*" In Olander and Greenberg 55–82.

Halberstam, David. *The Fifties.* New York: Villard, 1993.

Jacobs, Robert, "The Writer's Digest Interview." *The Writer's Digest* 55 (Feb. 1976): 18–25.

Johnson, Wayne L. *Ray Bradbury.* New York: Frederick Ungar, 1980.

Lamont, Lansing. *Day of Trinity.* New York: Atheneum, 1965.

McNelly, Willis E. "Two Views." In Olander and Greenberg 17–24.

Mogen, David. *Ray Bradbury.* Boston: Twayne, 1986.

Olander, Joseph D., and Martin Harry Greenberg, eds. *Ray Bradbury.* New York: Taplinger, 1980.

Oppenheimer, J. Robert. *The Open Mind.* New York: Simon and Schuster, 1955.

Pell, Sarah-Warner J. "Style is the Man: Imagery in Bradbury's Fiction." In Olander and Greenberg 186–94.

Rhodes, Richard. *The Making of the Atomic Bomb.* New York: Simon and Schuster, 1986.

Sisario, Peter. "A Study of the Allusions in Bradbury's *Fahrenheit 451*." *English Journal* 59 (1970): 201–05, 212.

Theoharis, Athan. *Seeds of Repression: Harry S. Truman and the Origins of McCarthyism.* Chicago: Quadrangle, 1971.

Touponce, William F. *Ray Bradbury.* Starmont Reader's Guide 31. Mercer Island, WA: Starmont House, 1989.

Watt, Donald. "Burning Bright: *Fahrenheit 451* as Symbolic Dystopia." In Olander and Greenberg 195–213.

Wolfe, Gary. *The Known and the Unknown: The Iconography of Science Fiction.* Kent, OH: Kent State UP, 1979.

Problems Warned About in *Fahrenheit 451* Threaten Today's World

Richard Widmann

Drawing comparisons between the firemen's actions in *Fahrenheit 451* and attacks on contemporary real-world authors and publishers of controversial subject matter, Richard Widmann charges that the fictional world Bradbury portrayed is now, in some frightening ways, fact. Censorship and even book burnings—the types of dangers Bradbury's novel warned against—already threaten today's supposedly democratic societies. Widmann writes widely on issues raised by the attempt to revise historical records to match lately discovered facts ("revisionism").

In 1952, Harry Elmer Barnes wrote a timely article, "How *'Nineteen Eighty-Four'* Trends Threaten American Peace, Freedom, and Prosperity," as the final chapter of the classic revisionist anthology, *Perpetual War for Perpetual Peace.* Barnes analyzed George Orwell's classic novel as a work of prophecy and sounded the alarm to reverse the *"1984"* trends prevalent in the America of his day. Barnes argued that propagandists and "court historians" were fashioning a present, based on a falsified and inaccurate telling of the past, that was designed to meet Establishment desires to participate in world wars. Ironically, Barnes' article was omitted from the first edition of the collection.

Barnes may be best remembered as the author of the generally accepted definition of "revisionism,"

> Revisionism means nothing more or less than the effort to correct the historical record in the light of a more complete

Reprinted from Richard Widmann, "How *Fahrenheit 451* Trends Threaten Intellectual Freedom," web article at www.codoh.com/F451.html, by permission of the author. (See website for complete list of references cited.)

collection of historical facts, a more calm political atmosphere, and a more objective attitude.[1]

Barnes had discovered that a more nearly accurate version of the history of the First World War was only possible after the fighting had ended and the emotional excesses had lessened. He was unable to predict that similar corrections of Allied propaganda and popularized conceptions of the methods of warfare in the Second World War would meet even sterner resistance.

Today—half a century after the conclusion of the Second World War—it would be fair to expect a less emotional environment, one in which historians, researchers and writers were free to examine the actual causes of the war as well as the atrocities committed by both sides in the conflict. However, those and other topics are more forbidden than ever with the greatest taboo surrounding analysis of the fate of Europe's Jews and others in what has come to be known as the Holocaust.

In 1950, three years prior to Barnes' article concerning *"1984"* trends, another author, Ray Bradbury, set out a foreboding vision of the future in a short story titled "The Fireman." Later, Bradbury's story would be [lengthened and] renamed *Fahrenheit 451* after the temperature at which paper burns. *Fahrenheit 451* describes a horrific future in which millions of books are banned and firemen set fires instead of extinguishing them. In order to maintain a society of brainwashed, "happy" people, the firemen kick down doors and burn the hated volumes along with the homes that housed them.

Barnes would never have suspected how fast the world would progress from the *"1984"* trends he identified to the trends Bradbury identified in *Fahrenheit 451*. In our time, we see the events of Bradbury's science fiction novel coming to pass every day.

CUSTODIANS OF OUR PEACE OF MIND

Bradbury explained the origins of the book burnings in *Fahrenheit 451* through his fire chief, Captain Beatty.

> "It didn't come from the Government down. There was no dictum, no declaration, no censorship, to start with, no! Technology, mass exploitation, and minority pressure carried the

---

1. Harry E. Barnes, "Revisionism and the Promotion of Peace," in *Barnes Against the Blackout*, p. 273. Barnes's article originally appeared in the Summer 1958 issue of *Liberation*.

trick, thank God. Today, thanks to them, you can stay happy all the time, you are allowed to read comics, the good old confessions, or trade journals."

Contemporary America is similarly undergoing a period of "political correctness" that has touched us on every societal level. The impulse not to "offend" has resulted in the censorship of thought which breaches the limits of recently defined "good taste." The solution to politically incorrect thought is obvious in Bradbury's nightmare world. In the words of Captain Beatty:

> "Colored people don't like *Little Black Sambo.* Burn it. White people don't feel good about *Uncle Tom's Cabin.* Burn it."

One of the first examples of a *"Fahrenheit 451"* trend was an arson-attack on The Historical Review Press (HRP), a publisher of revisionist books in Britain. On November 5, 1980, "firemen" destroyed the office, warehouse and printing plant of the HRP. Damage was estimated at 50,000 pounds. HRP rebuilt only to have the "firemen" return in September 1996. The offices were once again badly damaged by the "firemen's" flames.

HRP was not the only revisionist publisher to meet a fiery fate. On July 4,1984, "firemen" paid a call on the Institute for Historical Review (IHR) in California. IHR publishes revisionist histories of the Second World War and has dared to question elements of the orthodox "Holocaust" story. The "firemen" chose to attack IHR's warehouse and burn tens of thousands of books that they feared people would read. Among the books burned was Barnes' *Perpetual War for Perpetual Peace.*

On May 8, 1995, "firemen" in Canada brought their form of censorship to Ernst Zündel, a small independent publisher. Zündel had run into trouble with the authorities in Canada for publishing a slender volume which dared to pose the question, *Did Six Million Really Die?* After years of state censorship, Zündel's home and office were severely damaged by fire after an unknown assailant doused the building with gasoline and set it ablaze. Witnesses reported seeing what Bradbury readers would have to call a "fireman" carrying a red gasoline canister to the front of Zündel's home, "gingerly like a bomb," and setting the fire.

The damage was extensive; many books and files were destroyed. The blazing roof collapsed into the building. What wasn't ruined by the flames was damaged by the water of the official fire brigade which flooded the lower floors.

The message was loud and clear: Publications that inspire thought on certain controversial topics are not allowed.

SETTING THE STRUCTURE TO BURN THE BOOKS

Sometimes, the "firemen" are able to carry out their objective—preventing books from being read—without actually consigning volumes to the flames. In 1996, St. Martin's Press decided to publish a biography of Hitler's propaganda minister, Joseph Goebbels, written by David Irving, a popular albeit controversial British historian.

St. Martin's Press publisher Thomas Dunne issued the following angry statement after receiving dozens of protests against his plans to publish Irving's *Goebbels: Mastermind of the Third Reich.*

> "A number of the calls we have received have expressed fury that we would publish a book by 'a man like David Irving' and have questioned our moral right to do so. I can only say that Joseph Goebbels must be laughing in hell. He, after all, was the man who loved nothing better than burning books, threatening publishers, suppressing ideas and judging the merits of ideas based not on their content but by their author's racial, ethnic or political purity. That is indeed a sad irony."

The campaign to ban the book built for several weeks. Initially, St. Martin's editors stood by their decision and insisted they found nothing wrong with Irving's book. However, the pressure increased—now including death threats from the "firemen"—and Thomas McCormack, chief executive officer of St. Martin's, finally gave in and reversed the company's earlier position. St. Martin's decided not to publish Irving's volume. Far from being widely condemned, the St. Martin's surrender was upheld by numerous American newspapers.

Presumably St. Martin's Press would have acquiesced in a literal as well as a figurative incineration. Submitting to such tyranny is always simpler than standing up to it. In Bradbury's novel, Faber, a retired professor says,

> "I saw the way things were going, a long time back. I said nothing. I'm one of the innocents who could have spoken up and out when no one would listen to the 'guilty,' but I did not speak and thus became guilty myself. And when finally they set the structure to burn the books, using the firemen, I grunted a few times and subsided, for there were no others grunting or yelling with me, by then."

"Fahrenheit 451" trends are perhaps most prevalent in

Germany. Günther Deckert, a school teacher, translated into German a work of American execution consultant Fred Leuchter, titled *The Leuchter Report*. The report is Leuchter's 1988 analysis of the alleged gas chambers of Auschwitz and Majdanek. Deckert, who was very familiar with Leuchter's work, interpreted at a meeting at which Leuchter spoke in Weinheim in November of 1991.

For those actions, Deckert was dragged into court and given a one-year suspended sentence. Owing to protests over that "lenient" penalty, he was retried. This time, in a Karlsruhe court, Judge Eva-Marie Wollentin sentenced him to two years' imprisonment—in what has been described as "the freest state in German history."

The *Neue Osnabruecker Zeitung* spoke for many of Germany's modern editors in an editorial, intoning that it was a just sentence. "There was no reason to suspend the sentence passed on the rightwinger," it declared. "Deckert showed not the slightest repentance." In that, the newspaper was correct. When accused of having shared Leuchter's views, Deckert told the court: "I stand unconditionally by what I said."

Burn It!

"*Fahrenheit 451*" trends become most apparent after Germar Rudolf published an anthology titled *Grundlagen zur Zeitgeschichte: Ein Handbuch über strittige Fragen des 20. Jahrhunderts* (*Foundations of Contemporary History: A Handbook on Controversial Questions of the Twentieth Century*). Rudolf, forced to use pseudonyms after publishing *Das Rudolf Gutachten* (*The Rudolf Report*), his own scientific analysis of the purported Auschwitz gas chambers, suffered numerous raids on his home by the German state "firemen." In March of 1995, the "firemen" raided a German publisher and seized all available copies of *Grundlagen zur Zeitgeschichte*.

In May 1996, Judge Burckhardt Stein ruled that Rudolf had to be arrested without delay for his part in publishing the book. On June 15, 1996, the judge ruled that all copies of *Grundlagen zur Zeitgeschichte* must be burned. The "firemen" no longer had to operate under the cover of darkness— they were now given official authority to carry out their murder of ideas. Not content to simply burn the words of Rudolf and his co-authors, the "firemen" sentenced Rudolf to 14 months' imprisonment. He has so far eluded his captors and today writes in exile.

In Bradbury's novel, Captain Beatty discovers that Montag, the novel's hero—and a renegade fireman—had hidden books in his home. For that infraction, the "firemen" visit Montag's home and Beatty orders Montag to burn his own books.

> "I want you to do this job all by your lonesome, Montag. Not with kerosene and a match, but piecework, with a flame thrower. Your house, your clean-up."

As Montag burns his home and precious books, Beatty declares, not unlike Judge Stein,

> "When you're quite finished . . . you're under arrest."

These are not isolated cases. In February 1995, after receiving numerous complaints, a German publisher ordered the "recycling" of John Sack's *An Eye for an Eye*, which recounts the story of Jewish revenge against the Germans after World War II. Citing information from Germany's Federal Archives, Sack, who is himself Jewish, maintains that 60,000 to 80,000 ethnic Germans were killed or otherwise perished between 1945 and 1948 in camps run by the Polish communist regime's Office of State Security.

The German cultural establishment launched a bitter assault. The book was denounced as a sensationalist, "vile docudrama" and a "gift to neo-Nazis." Soon, the book's publisher, R. Piper, found itself deluged with complaints.

All 6,000 copies of the German edition were stacked in a Stuttgart warehouse when Piper publisher Viktor Niemann decided to destroy them. On February 13, the publisher announced, "They will be recycled."

In December of 1996, German authorities ordered all copies of Carlos Porter's *Not Guilty at Nuremberg: The German Defense Case* to be destroyed along with the means of reproducing it. Porter resided in Belgium at the time of the German order. Porter's troubles with the German thought police began in August 1996 when he sent several copies of his book, along with a cover letter, to several people in Germany.

In Munich, a certain Judge Zeilinger ruled that Porter had violated the German law against "defamation and desecration." He was fined 6,000 DM for writing and distributing his book, which is a revisionist analysis of the Nuremberg trials. Zeilinger also directed, in her "Order of Punishment," that all copies of *Not Guilty at Nuremberg* be confiscated, including copies in Porter's personal possession. Zeilinger wrote: "It is also ordered that all means for the production of this published work be confiscated, including any plates, forms, templates, negatives, or matrices."

Zeilinger charged that various passages from Porter's revisionist analysis denied or minimized the tales of the "Holocaust."

STRIKING THE MATCH

One of the most moving scenes in Bradbury's novel is the raid on an old woman's home when neighbors tip off the authorities that she has built an illegal library. The "firemen" squirt their kerosene over the books. Montag later explains to his wife, "We burnt copies of Dante and Swift and Marcus Aurelius." When the "firemen" attempt to drag the old woman from her house, she refuses to cooperate. The woman is too proud to give in to the "firemen" and instead carries out the final act of rebellion by striking a match and immolating herself.

> "On the front porch where she had come to weigh them quietly with her eyes, her quietness a condemnation, the woman stood motionless. Beatty flicked his fingers to spark the kerosene. He was too late. Montag gasped. The woman on the porch reached out with contempt to them all and struck the kitchen match against the railing."

In April 1995, Reinhold Elstner, a former Wehrmacht soldier, chose the same miserable fate. He wrote in his final letter:

> A Niagra of lies and defamations inundates us. Since I am now 75 years old, there is not much left for me to do—but I can still seek death by self-immolation; one last deed that may act as a signal to the Germans to come to their senses. Even if through my deed only one German will awaken, and because of it will find the way to the truth, then my sacrifice will not have been in vain. I felt I have no other choice once I realized that even now, after 50 years, there seems to be little hope that reason would gain the upper hand.

Elstner went to the *Feldherrnhalle* memorial hall in downtown Munich and poured gasoline over himself and struck a match. Authorities have banned the publication of his letter and have even made it illegal to leave flowers for Elstner at the site of his immolation. Many wonder how long it would have been before Germany's "firemen" visited Elstner had he not preempted them.

CONCLUSIONS

Today authors around the world are finding publishers afraid to touch their manuscripts. Brave publishers are finding printers shutting down their presses to controversial volumes. Published volumes are being consigned to sanctioned burnings by the "firemen."

Around the world, news of immolations like Elstner's is blacked out. We are supposed to occupy our minds with sports on big-screen TV's, video arcades, fast food, cellular telephones to occupy our minds while traveling, laptop computers and even on-flight computer games. Computerized "chat rooms" that enable us to "speak" to faceless strangers are all the rage. How far are we from Bradbury's broadcast TV "families"? Montag's wife exclaims, "if we had a fourth wall [of wall-size TV screens], why it'd be just like this room wasn't ours at all, but all kinds of exotic people's rooms."

When war is declared in *Fahrenheit 451*, people are not over concerned. It will be a "quick war. Forty-eight hours, they said, and everyone home. That's what the Army said." Recall President Clinton's promise that American troops would be home from Bosnia by September 1996! No one seems to mind that they have yet to return. Actual thought is indeed rare today, perhaps because it is so frowned upon.

How many readers of this article have hidden their books and journals? Have you established a secret library yet? Are you afraid of your friends and loved ones? Guy Montag hid his books:

> He reached up and pulled back the grille of the air-conditioning system and reached far back inside to the right and moved still another sliding sheet of metal and took out a book.

Such hiding places are something that each of us should consider if the *"Fahrenheit 451"* trends prevalent today are not reversed.

Ironically, Bradbury mentions censorship of his book on censorship in the "Coda" of *Fahrenheit 451.*

> I discovered that, over the years, some cubby-hole editors at Ballantine Books, fearful of contaminating the young, had, bit by bit, censored some 75 separate sections from the novel.

Let there be no mistake—the "firemen" are actively at large and active. Our future depends on truth and intellectual freedom rising phoenix-like from the ashes of the present.

Chronology

1920

Raymond Douglas Bradbury is born in Waukegan, Illinois, August 22. Responding to fears of communist domination, the United States becomes caught up in a "Red hunt"; Attorney General A. Mitchell Palmer authorizes raids on private houses and labor headquarters without warrants; President Woodrow Wilson pleads, "Do not let the country see Red."

1928

Given a copy of *Amazing Stories,* Bradbury begins a lifelong fascination with science fiction.

1931

Bradbury begins writing his first stories.
Chicago World's Fair.

1934

Bradbury family moves to Los Angeles, where they will remain.

1938

Bradbury's first short story, "Hollerbochen's Dilemma," is published in *Imagination!* magazine. On May 26, the U.S. House of Representatives sets up a committee to investigate "un-American" activities; originally charged with investigating those of both the political left and the right, it eventually will concentrate on the left, which it believes has communist sympathies.

1939

Bradbury publishes four issues of his own science fiction fan magazine, *Futuria Fantasia.* He attends the first World Science Fiction Convention in New York City.

1943

Bradbury begins to sell work steadily (eleven stories will sell this year, eighteen in 1944). Most editors reject his type of science fiction, so he tries writing for mystery magazines.

1944

Publishes several stories in pulp detective magazines, including *New Detective, Detective Tales,* and *Dime Mystery.*

1946

Bradbury meets Marguerite Susan ("Maggie") McClure, a clerk at Fowler's Bookshop in downtown Los Angeles.

1947

Bradbury and McClure marry. His first book, *Dark Carnival,* a collection of short horror stories, is published. He begins selling material to the CBS radio show *Suspense.* He writes "The Phoenix," which he will later develop into the short story "The Fireman," which will eventually become *Fahrenheit 451.* On October 20, the House Un-American Activities Committee (HUAC) opens public hearings on alleged communist infiltration of Hollywood. For its "Hollywood Hearings," HUAC has three goals: to prove that the Screen Writers' Guild has communist members; that these writers have inserted subversive propaganda into Hollywood films; and, according to J. Parnell Thomas, head of the committee, that President Roosevelt encouraged pro-Soviet films during the war. None of these claims is substantiated, but the attack forces many talented and creative people to leave Hollywood.

1949

Bradbury's first daughter, Susan Marguerite, is born November 5. The National Fantasy Fan Federation selects him as science fiction and fantasy's "best author of 1949."

1950

Bradbury publishes *The Martian Chronicles.* President Truman instructs the Atomic Energy Commission to produce the hydrogen bomb, which will have far greater destructive potential than the atomic bombs dropped on Japan in WW II.

1951

Bradbury's second daughter, Ramone Anne, is born May 17.

He publishes *The Illustrated Man.* His short story "The Fireman" is published in the February issue of *Galaxy Science Fiction.*

1953

Bradbury publishes *Golden Apples of the Sun* and *Fahrenheit 451.* Arthur Miller's new play, *The Crucible,* seemingly about the Salem witch trials of 1692 (when the hysterical accusations of a few young Massachusetts girls led to the executions of twenty people for witchcraft), is actually a commentary on the "witch hunts" Senator Joseph McCarthy and others are conducting through such means as Senate hearings (using tactics similar to those of the House Un-American Activities Committee) and the jailing of those either accused of being communists or accused of refusing to denounce others as communists.

1954

A serialized version of *Fahrenheit 451* appears in the March, April, and May 1954 issues of *Playboy* magazine. On December 2, the U.S. Senate censures Senator Joseph McCarthy for his insults to fellow senators and accusations of treason against army officials, for indiscriminately accusing people of being communists without proof and designating guilt by association, and for contempt of a Senate committee investigating his conduct and financial affairs. With this censure, he is stripped of his powers to continue his investigation of supposed communist subversion.

1955

Bradbury's third daughter, Bettina Francion, is born July 22.

1956

"Shopping for Death," Bradbury's first of several TV plays for the *Alfred Hitchcock Show,* airs in January.

1957

Bradbury publishes *Dandelion Wine,* a fictionalized treatment of his childhood in Waukegan, Illinois, which he calls Green Town.

1958

Bradbury's fourth daughter, Alexandra Allison, is born August 13.

1959

Bradbury publishes *A Medicine for Melancholy.*

1962

Bradbury publishes *Something Wicked This Way Comes* (another book based on his Waukegan childhood) and *R Is for Rocket.*

1963

Icarus Montgolfier Wright, an eighteen-minute animated film based on Bradbury's short story of the same name, is nominated for an Academy Award as best animated short subject of the year; he shares the screenplay credit with George C. Johnson. (Although he does not win the Oscar, he does receive the Golden Eagle Film Award from the Council on International Nontheatrical Events for the film.) His first drama collection, *The Anthem Sprinters and Other Antics,* is published.

1964

Bradbury's *The Machineries of Joy* is published. He is commissioned to write *An American Journey,* a film history of the country, for the U.S. government pavilion at the New York World's Fair.

1966

Director François Truffaut's film version of *Fahrenheit 451* is released. Simon and Schuster issues a new edition of the book with a new introduction by Bradbury.

1969

The film *The Illustrated Man* is released, based on three stories from Bradbury's book of the same name. Publishes *I Sing the Body Electric!*

1972

Publishes *The Wonderful Ice Cream Suit and Other Plays* and *The Halloween Tree.*

1973

Bradbury publishes first collection of poetry, *When Elephants Last in the Dooryard Bloomed.*

1975

Bradbury publishes *Pillar of Fire and Other Plays.*

1976

Bradbury publishes *Long After Midnight.*

1977

Bradbury publishes second poetry collection, *Where Robot Mice and Robot Men Run Round in Robot Towns.* He receives Life Achievement Award at the World Fantasy Convention.

1980

Bradbury publishes *The Stories of Ray Bradbury.*

1981

Bradbury publishes *The Haunted Computer and the Android Pope*, his third collection of poetry.

1982

Bradbury publishes *The Complete Poems of Ray Bradbury.*

1983

Bradbury publishes *Dinosaur Tales.*

1984

The movie *Something Wicked This Way Comes*, with Bradbury's screenplay (based on his 1962 book of the same name), is released. He publishes *A Memory of Murder,* an anthology of some of his early mystery stories. The Libertarian Futurist Society gives him its Prometheus Hall of Fame Award for Best Classic Libertarian Science-Fiction Novel, for *Fahrenheit 451.*

1985

Bradbury publishes *Death Is a Lonely Business.*

1988

The Science Fiction and Fantasy Writers of America give Bradbury the Grand Master Nebula Award.

1990

Bradbury publishes *A Graveyard for Lunatics* and *Zen in the Art of Writing.*

1991

Bradbury publishes a collection of essays, *Yestermorrow: Obvious Answers to Impossible Futures.*

1992

Bradbury publishes *Green Shadows, White Whale.*

1996

Bradbury publishes *Quicker than the Eye.*

1997

Bradbury publishes *Driving Blind,* a collection of stories, and two poems bound as books: *Dogs Think That Every Day Is Christmas* and *With Cat for Comforter.*

1998

Bradbury publishes *Ahmed and the Oblivion Machines: A Fable.*

1999

Journey to Far Metaphor, a collection of essays on the art and craft of writing, is forthcoming from Capra Press.

For Further Research

E.F. Bleiler, ed., *Science Fiction Writers: Critical Studies of the Major Authors from the Early Nineteenth Century to the Present Day.* New York: Scribner, 1982.

Ray Bradbury, "The Day After Tomorrow: Why Science Fiction?" *Nation,* May 2, 1953.

———, "A Rationale for Bookburners: A Further Word from Ray Bradbury," *ALA Bulletin,* May 1961.

———, *Zen in the Art of Writing.* Santa Barbara, CA: Capra Press, 1990.

August Derleth, review of *Fahrenheit 451, Chicago Sunday Tribune,* October 15, 1953.

Martin Harry Greenberg and Joseph D. Olander, *Ray Bradbury.* New York: Taplinger, 1980.

Wayne L. Johnson, *Ray Bradbury.* New York: Frederick Ungar, 1980.

David Mogen, *Ray Bradbury.* Boston: Twayne, 1986.

Sam Moskowitz, *Seekers of Tomorrow: Masters of Modern Science Fiction.* Cleveland and New York: World, 1966.

William F. Nolan, "Ray Bradbury: Prose Poet in the Age of Space," *Magazine of Fantasy and Science Fiction,* May 1963.

———, *The Ray Bradbury Companion.* Detroit: Gale Research, 1975.

William F. Nolan and Martin H. Greenberg, eds., *The Bradbury Chronicles: Stories in Honor of Ray Bradbury.* New York: ROC, 1991.

Eric S. Rabkin, Martin H. Greenberg, and Joseph D. Olander, eds., *No Place Else: Explorations in Utopian and Dystopian Fiction.* Carbondale and Edwardsville: Southern Illinois University Press, 1983.

Peter Sisario, "A Study of the Allusions in Bradbury's *Fahrenheit 451*," *English Journal,* February 1970.

George Edgar Slusser, *The Bradbury Chronicles.* Milford Series Popular Writers of Today. San Bernardino, CA: Borgo Press, 1977.

William F. Touponce, *Ray Bradbury.* Mercer Island, WA: Starmont House, 1989.

———, *Ray Bradbury and the Poetics of Reverie: Fantasy, Science Fiction, and the Reader.* Ann Arbor, MI: UMI Research Press, 1984.

INTERESTING EDITIONS OF *FAHRENHEIT 451*

Ray Bradbury has written a Foreword (1993), an Introduction (1967), an Afterword (1982), and a Coda (1979) for *Fahrenheit 451.* Various editions of the book contain one or more of these writings; for example, the Del Rey paperback editions printed after 1982 contain the Afterword and the Coda; Simon and Schuster's 40th Anniversary hardcover edition of 1993 contains the Introduction and the new Foreword. A special limited-edition version of the book with an asbestos cover was printed in 1953. The short story which Bradbury later expanded into the novel *Fahrenheit 451,* was originally published in *Galaxy Science Fiction,* vol. 1, no. 5 (February 1951), under the title "The Fireman."

THEMES AND HISTORICAL BACKGROUND

A. J. Anderson, *Problems in Intellectual Freedom and Censorship.* New York: Bowker, 1974.

Jack Anderson and Ronald W. May, *McCarthy: The Man, the Senator, the "ism."* Boston: Beacon Press, 1952.

Paul Blanshard, *The Right to Read: The Battle Against Censorship.* Boston: Beacon Press, 1955.

William F. Buckley Jr., and L. Brent Bozell, *McCarthy and His Enemies: The Record and Its Meaning.* Chicago: H. Regnery, 1954. Reissued 1995.

Lee Burress, *Battle of the Books: Literary Censorship in the Public Schools, 1950–1985.* Metuchen, NJ: Scarecrow Press, 1989.

Roy M. Cohn, *McCarthy.* New York: New American Library, 1968.

Walter M. Daniels, *The Censorship of Books.* New York: Wilson, 1954.

Robert Bingham Downs, *The First Freedom: Liberty and Justice in the World of Books and Reading.* Chicago: American Library Association, 1960.

John H. Ferres, ed., *Twentieth Century Interpretations of* The Crucible: *A Collection of Critical Essays.* Englewood Cliffs, NJ: Prentice-Hall, 1972.

Albert Fried, ed., *McCarthyism: The Great American Red Scare: A Documentary History.* New York: Oxford University Press, 1997.

Richard M. Fried, *Nightmare in Red: The McCarthy Era in Perspective.* New York: Oxford University Press, 1990.

Earl Latham, *The Meaning of McCarthyism,* 2nd ed. Lexington, MA: D.C. Heath, 1973.

Owen Lattimore, *Ordeal by Slander.* Boston: Little, Brown, 1950.

Seymour J. Mandelbaum, *The Social Setting of Intolerance: The Know-Nothings, the Red Scare, and McCarthyism.* Chicago: Scott, Foresman, 1964.

Karl Marx, *On Freedom of the Press and Censorship.* Translated and with an introduction by Saul K. Padover. New York: McGraw-Hill, 1974.

William Noble, *Bookbanning in America: Who Bans Books?—and Why?* Middlebury, VT: P.S. Eriksson, 1990.

Office for Intellectual Freedom of the American Library Association, comp., *Intellectual Freedom Manual,* 5th ed. Chicago: American Library Association, 1996.

David M. Oshinsky, *A Conspiracy So Immense: The World of Joe McCarthy.* New York: Free Press, 1983.

Henry Reichman, *Censorship and Selection: Issues and Answers for Schools.* Chicago: American Library Association; Arlington, VA: American Association of School Administrators, 1993.

Louise S. Robbins, *Censorship and the American Library: The American Library Association's Response to Threats to Intellectual Freedom, 1939–1969.* Westport, CT: Greenwood, 1996.

Michael Paul Rogin, *The Intellectuals and McCarthy: The Radical Specter.* Cambridge, MA: MIT Press, 1967.

Ellen Schrecker, *The Age of McCarthyism: A Brief History with Documents.* Boston: Bedford Books of St. Martin's Press, 1994. (For an online excerpt, see www.crocker.com/~blklist/bibliog.html)

————, *Many Are the Crimes: McCarthyism in America.* Boston: Little, Brown, 1998.

Victoria Sherrow, *Censorship in Schools.* Springfield, NJ: Enslow, 1996.

Byron Stay, ed., *Censorship: Opposing Viewpoints.* San Diego, CA: Greenhaven Press, 1997.

Carol Wekesser, ed., *Pornography: Opposing Viewpoints.* San Diego, CA: Greenhaven Press, 1997.

Mark I. West, *Trust Your Children: Voices Against Censorship in Children's Literature.* New York: Neal-Schuman, 1997.

INDEX